Journal across the Plains, 1852

This book is dedicated to yesterday's pioneers who braved the journey across the plains and to tomorrow's pioneers, as they seek future frontiers.

JOURNAL ACROSS THE PLAINS, 1852

THE BROTHERS VERDENAL, MISSOURI TO CALIFORNIA

JOHN MARTIN VERDENAL AND
DOMINIQUE FRANÇOIS VERDENAL

EDITED BY JO M. HARAF

AMERICA
THROUGH TIME®
ADDING COLOR TO AMERICAN HISTORY

America Through Time is an imprint of Fonthill Media LLC
www.through-time.com
office@through-time.com

Published by Arcadia Publishing by arrangement with Fonthill Media LLC
For all general information, please contact Arcadia Publishing:
Telephone: 843-853-2070
Fax: 843-853-0044
E-mail: sales@arcadiapublishing.com
For customer service and orders:
Toll-Free 1-888-313-2665
Visit us on the internet at www.arcadiapublishing.com

First published 2020

ISBN 978-1-63499-273-2

Typeset in Mrs Eaves XL Serif Narrow 10pt on 13pt
Printed and bound in England

Contents

ACKNOWLEDGMENTS

From April into October 1852, the Verdenal family traveled from St. Louis, Missouri, to Placerville, California—a journey of six months and two thousand miles. By comparison, this book's journey from concept to publication consumed two years and no miles to speak of unless you count our authors' steps from research to keyboard. Like the El Dorado wagon train, the *Journal's* publication team included a full roster of active contributors:

Heather Powell, Marin History Museum's (MHM) Collections Manager, launched the *Journal* when she shared the original diary with the museum's volunteer team. Heather documented the Verdenal family's artifacts in photographs, scans, and acquisition research. Heather contributed mightily to the photography and illustration research.

Jo Haraf led our publication train. While one member of the El Dorado train threatened his wagon master at gunpoint, Jo thankfully found her traveling companions dependably good-humored and collegial.

Brian Crawford served as our journey's extraordinary biographer, photo sleuth, and mapmaker. His detailed research and biographies added authenticity and weight to the boys' story. Mary Rostad translated Brian's carefully plotted digital maps into the *Journal's* printed versions that trace the Verdenal family journey.

Other invaluable train members include editors Jean Harkee Mansen and Larry A. Paul as well as Catherine Conway Honig for her French translations. We are grateful they joined us on our journey.

This book would not exist if not for the foresight and generosity of exceptional supporters. Ann Batman proposed this book to the Marin History Museum's Board of Directors, pledging not only her attention but financial support to see the *Journal* through to publication. Dewitt K. "Ken" and Mary Margaret "Dolly" McDonald (a descendant of John Martin Verdenal Sr.) donated her great-grandfather's original handwritten diary as well as other family artifacts to the museum. Our gratitude to Ann, Ken, and Dolly spans the continent.

Finally, Ann Batman funded this project in memory of her husband, Richard Batman, western historian extraordinaire.

Editor's Notes and Resources

Although observant and articulate authors, the Verdenal brothers wrote in the style of the 1800s. Understandably, their spelling, punctuation, and capitalization patterns do not comply with today's standards. As editors, we strove for readability while retaining the boys' unique voices. To that end, the printed transcript follows these standards:

- Period capitalization (e.g. Buffalo, Antelope, Beans, Rice...) has been retained.
- Light punctuation has been inserted for readability.
- *Journal* entry dates are recreated as written.
- Errors in grammar (i.e. "they brang..."), spelling (i.e. "Wether cool & pleasant."), omissions (i.e. "He a wife in the train but no children."), and abbreviations (i.e. "acct" for "account") are retained.
- Undecipherable words are enclosed in brackets. "Wagon No 8, the unlucky tar wagon, in descending the bank [precipated] Mrs. James, an Irish lady, in the river." Brackets are also used for additional editorial information. "at noon reached the Humboldt river [*they had now entered Nevada*]."

A variety of online and hard copy resources assisted us in the creation of this book. We are grateful to those who preceded us on the trail and left their knowledge for us.

- Ancestry.com
- Newspapers.com
- California Digital Newspaper Collection www.cdnc.ucr.edu
- National Oregon/California Trail Center www.oregontrailcenter.org
- *Maps of the Oregon Trail*, Gregory M. Franzwa, The Patrice Press, Gerald, Missouri, 1982, 292 pages.

For additional information on the Verdenal family and the resources of the Marin History Museum, please visit www.MarinHistory.org.

(P. E.)

POLICE GÉNÉRALE
DE FRANCE.

Passe-port
à l'Etranger,
valable pour un an.

DÉPARTEMENT
du haut rhin

Registre 6ème
N° 1988.

SIGNALEMENT.

Agée de 16 ans
taille d'un mètre
50 centimètres
(pieds pouce),
cheveux noirs
front moyen
sourcils noirs
yeux bruns
nez petit
bouche moyenne
barbe
menton rond
visage long
teint clair

SIGNES PARTICULIERS.

Signature du Porteur :
françoise Reiset

Passe-port à l'Etranger,
Valable pour un an.

AU NOM DU ROI,

Nous Préfet du département du haut rhin

Requérons les Autorités civiles et militaires du Royaume, et prions les Autorités civiles et militaires des Etats amis ou alliés de la France, de laisser passer librement Melle Reiset, françoise, Couturière,
native de Id
demeurant à chavannes les Grands,
allant à New-york, (Amérique) pour s'y établir.
et de lui donner aide et protection en cas de besoin.

Le présent Passe-port est valable pendant
pour sortir du Royaume.

Fait à Colmar, le 16 Mai 1837.

Le Préfet.

Par le Préfet :
Le Conseiller de Préfecture
Secrétaire Général,

Prix du Passe-port : DIX FRANCS.

Françoise Reiset's Passport
[*Marin History Museum*]

Good-bye New York. Hello Missouri.

Surely John Martin and Dominique were not surprised when their father announced they were abandoning St. Louis for California. Leaving home for a distant land was a Verdenal family tradition.

In the early 1800s, the boys' future father, Jean Baptiste Verdenal Jr., left Alsace, a region in northeastern France bordering Germany, headed for the United States. Françoise Reiset, the young woman who would become their mother, also traveled from Alsace to America. Described in her 1837 passport as having black hair, brown eyes, and a fair complexion, sixteen-year-old Françoise demonstrated that she too had the courage to traverse an ocean in search of a better life.

Whether Jean Baptiste and Françoise knew each other in Alsace is unknown. Once in America, they fell in love and married on a cold Saturday in January 1839, at the still-under-construction St. Peter's Church in lower Manhattan. Like many immigrants whose names lost their old country spelling, Jean and Françoise's marriage certificate records their names as John and Frances. Although John Baptiste's reported birth date ranges from 1803 to 1808, he was at least a decade older than his bride.

The newly married couple settled in Utica, New York where their son, John Martin, was born eleven months later, in December 1839. The second and last of their sons, Dominique François, arrived in August 1841. Two years later, John Baptiste became a naturalized American citizen, certifying that he had been a resident of the United States for no less than five years and of New York state for at least one year. During the years surrounding John Baptiste's naturalization, Frances continued the family's wandering ways, taking a minimum of two trips back to France.

The same year John Baptiste became a citizen, explorer John Charles Fremont's second expedition documented the overland route to the Oregon territory, launching the country's great westward migration. Perhaps inspired by Fremont's expedition, the Verdenal family migrated over 800 miles southwest from Utica to St. Louis, Missouri, where John Martin

I certify. That John Baptiste Vaerdenal and Frances Reze were married by me on the 26th of January AD 1839. accordin to the rites and ceremonies of the Catholic Church.

New York January 26 1839.

Jno Power Rector of St Peters

[illegible]

Jean Baptiste and Françoise Verdenal's Marriage Certificate
[*Marin History Museum*]

and Dominique attended school. At over 100,000 residents, five times the size of Utica, St. Louis was a major hub for people migrating west to Oregon or California.

Over the coming years, the Verdenals watched friends and neighbors sell out and head west, seeking riches in gold or fertile farmland. Newspapers described the fortunes to be made on the other side of the continent. *The New York Tribune* reported how the steamship *Cherokee* had arrived in port bearing $2,000,000 in gold [$62,000,000 in 2019]. Closer to St. Louis, the *Palmyra Weekly Whig* ran a regular column toting up the millions of dollars of California gold being minted into double eagle coins at the Philadelphia Mint.

In 1852, John Baptiste was nearing fifty and Frances was in her early thirties. John Martin and Dominique were twelve and ten years old respectively, mature enough to care for themselves and perhaps even help during a westward migration. Although editorial

St. Louis, Missouri (1859)
[*Library of Congress/A. Janicke & Co.*]

writers warned that gold was not inexhaustible and that the tales of 96-pound gold lumps were "humbug," John Baptiste needed to move once again.

We can document little of what the family packed for their cross-continental trip. From family heirlooms, we know Frances carried her well-traveled French passport and marriage certificate, perhaps in a shoebox-sized, black tin box detailed in gold and red with VERDENAL etched in one side. One could imagine a bored boy, rocking in the back of a covered wagon, surrounded by what must have seemed like an infinity of prairie, scratching his name into the box.

Verdenal family lore suggests they also loaded an ornate child's bed and box spring into their wagon—an odd inclusion. With a headboard towering nearly six feet, the bed should have been too large for a cramped wagon pulled by burdened oxen. At less than four feet in length, the too-tall bed would have been too short for either boy. Still, the bed-that-crossed-the-country-in-a-covered-wagon was destined to be handed down through the Verdenal family as a treasured heirloom for five generations.

Finally, in the spring of 1852, the packing was done. The family, settled on their ox-harnessed wagon or riding horses, met their new traveling companions and began their six-month journey to California. All that was left was for John Martin and Dominique to record the tale.

Verdenal Tin Box
[*Marin History Museum*]

Verdenal Bed Frame
[*Marin History Museum*]

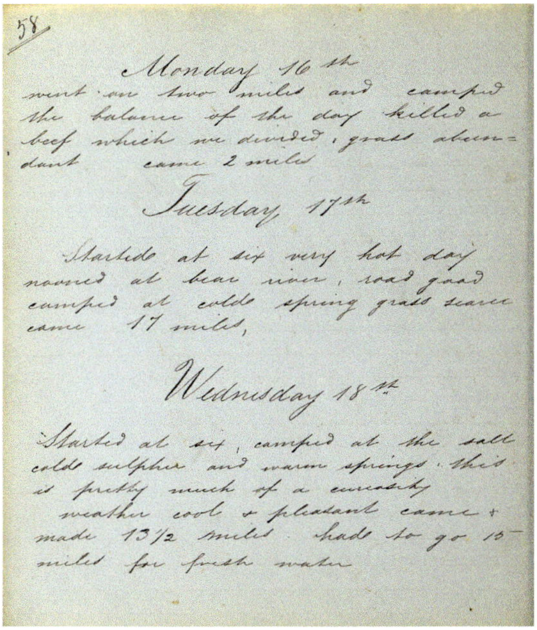

58

Monday 16th
went on two miles and camped the balance of the day killed a beef which we divided, grass abundant came 2 miles

Tuesday 17th
Started at six very hot day nooned at bear river, road good camped at cold spring grass scarce came 17 miles,

Wednesday 18th
Started at six, camped at the salt cold sulphur and warm springs. this is pretty much of a curiosity weather cool & pleasant came & made 13 1/2 miles had to go 15 miles for fresh water

Entries by John Martin Verdenal
[*Marin History Museum*]

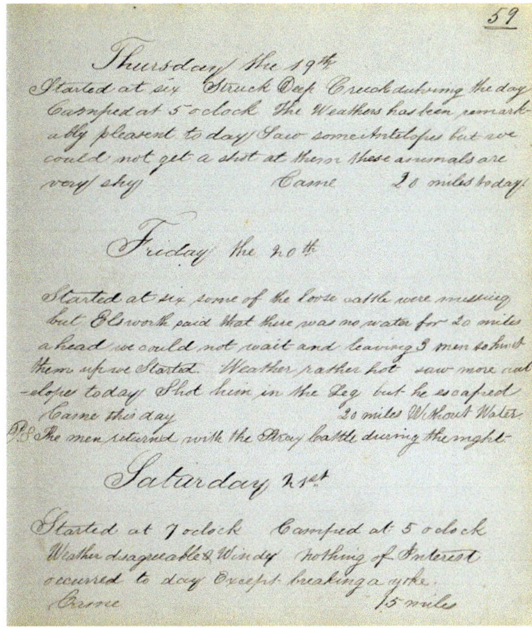

59

Thursday the 19th
Started at six Struck Deep Creek during the day Camped at 5 o clock the Weather has been remarkably pleasant to day Saw some Antelope but we could not get a shot at them these animals are very shy Came 20 miles to day

Friday the 20th
Started at six some of the loose cattle were missing but Elsworth said that there was no water for 20 miles a head we could not wait and leaving 3 men to hunt them up we Started Weather rather hot saw more antelope today Shot him in the Leg but he escaped Came this day 20 miles Without Water
P.S. The men returned with the Stray cattle during the night

Saturday 21st
Started at 7 oclock Camped at 5 o clock Weather disagreeable & Windy nothing of Interest occurred to day Except breaking a yoke. Came 15 miles

Entries by Dominique Françoise Verdenal
[*Marin History Museum*]

The journal in the museum's collection was written by two youthful hands, one prone to careful flourishes and the other casually scribed. From signatures and references, it is certain that the brothers Verdenal were the authors.

What is in doubt is exactly when the brothers wrote the journal. One version of events has the boys sitting by the nightly campfire, noting the events of the day in their small brown diary.

Another view suggests the museum's journal was written well after the journey's end based on notes the boys, and perhaps their parents, recorded en route. A few clues support the "written later" hypothesis. On the first day of the journey, John wrote that the train owner "had a tyrannical disposition," an opinion generally formed over days and weeks, not hours. The existing journal lacks the ink stains, dirt, watermarks, and other damage seen in similar cross-country diaries. Finally, in the journal's last entry, John is unable to remember the date he left Placerville for San Francisco. If the journal was written contemporaneously to the events of the day, surely he would have known the date of such a momentous move.

Perhaps the truth lies somewhere in between. Conceivably, the boys recorded the day's events in a journal while crossing the country. Then, once in California, they transcribed their original trail-weary diary into the neat volume now in the care of the Marin History Museum.

Regardless of the Journal's exact creation, John and Dominique's story remains an engaging retelling of six months spent traveling from St. Louis, Missouri to a new life and new adventures in California.

The brothers John Martin Verdenal and Dominique François Verdenal both wrote entries in the diaries.

The dates for Dominique's entries are:
April 26–30, 1852
May 1–6, 1852
May 15–19, 1852
August 19–25, 1852

The dates for John Martin's entries are:
May 7–14, 1852
May 20–31, 1852
June 1–30, 1852
July 1–31, 1852
August 1–18, 1852
August 26–31, 1852
September 1–30, 1852
October 1–12, 1852

As can be seen, the majority were written by the elder brother, John Martin Verdenal.

In reading the journal, the reader can refer to the accompanying detailed maps to see where the family was at the time. For clarity, the approximate positions of their camps are shown only once a week, along with significant landmarks.

Journal Cover
[*Marin History Museum*]

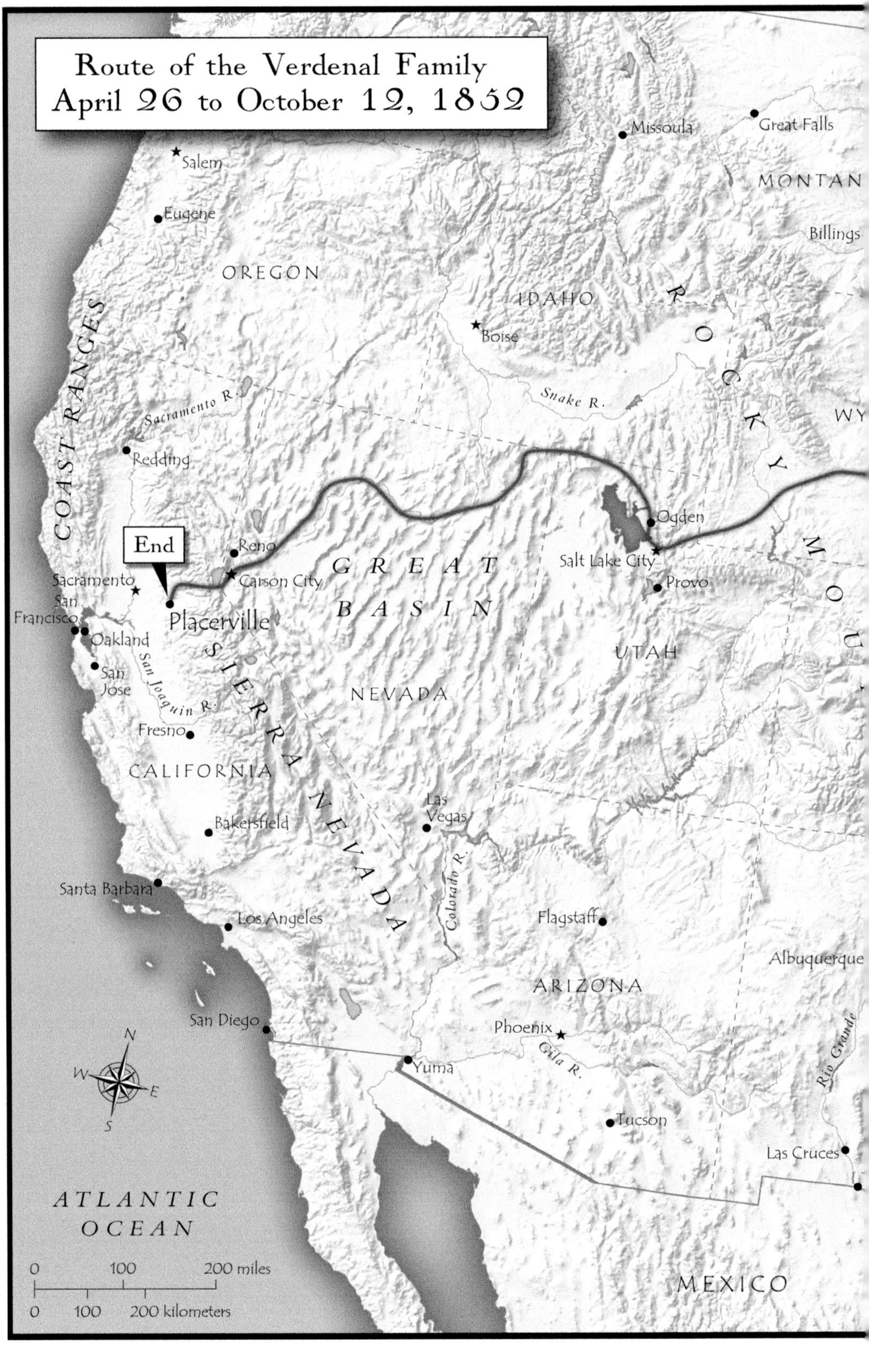

Route of the Verdenal Family
April 26 to October 12, 1852

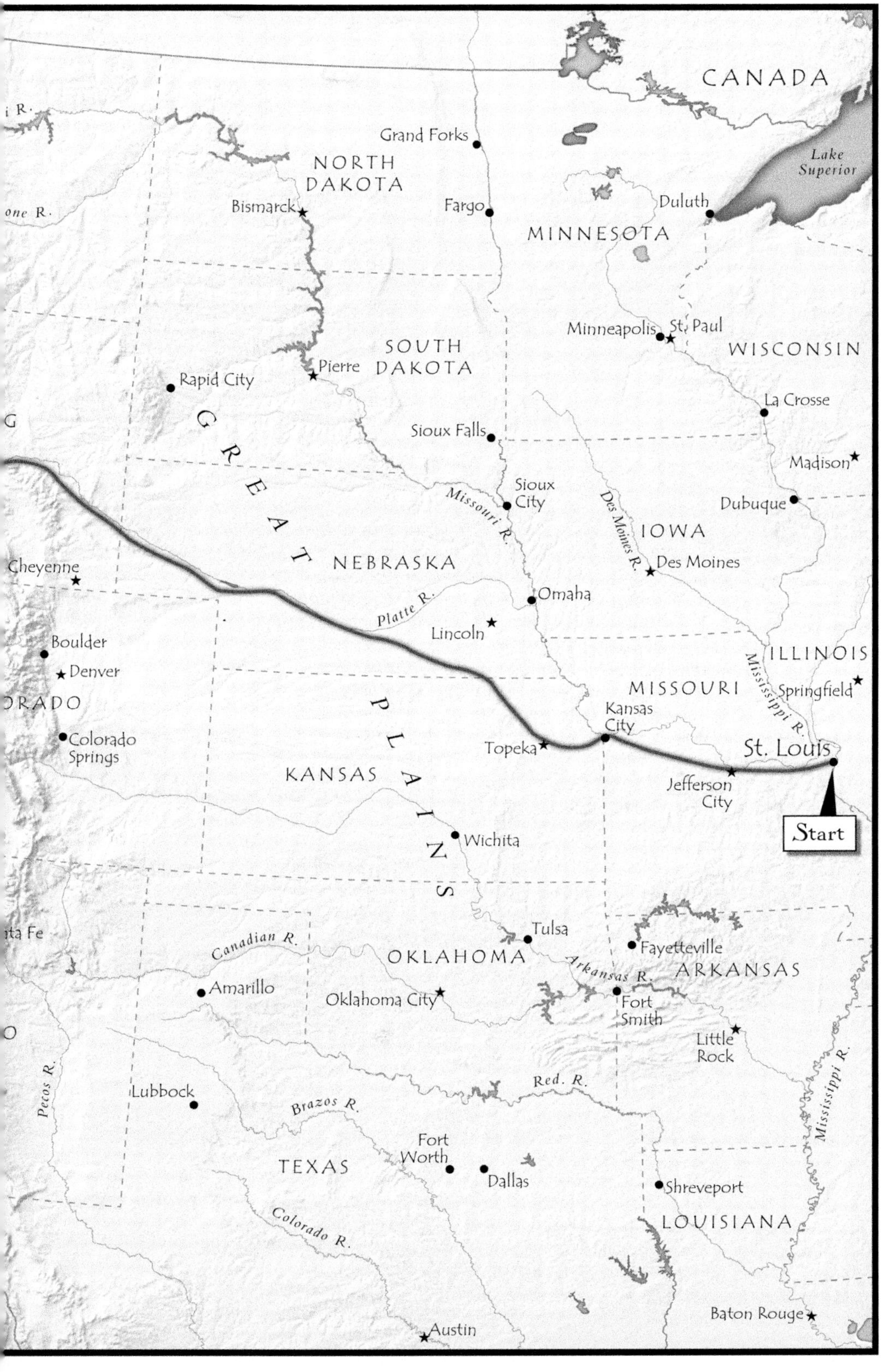

[Marin History Museum/Mary Rostad]

Journal Across the Plains

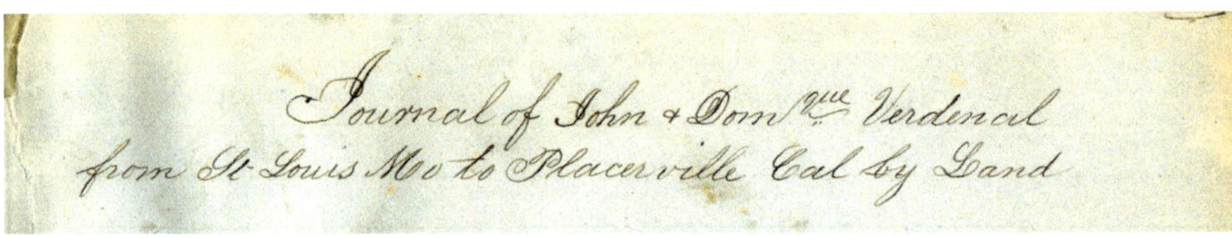
Journal of John & Dom^{que} Verdenal
from St Louis Mo to Placerville Cal by Land

[*Marin History Museum*]

Journal of John & Dom^{que} Verdenal
from Saint Louis Mo to Placerville Cal by Land

We Started from St Louis, Mo on Monday April 26th 1852 in the train of P. H. Elsworth for California. The train was called the "El Dorado Train",[1] it Consisted of 13 wagons (each wagon was numbered ours was No 4) and about 75 persons about 200 head of Cattle and 15 horses. Our provisions were as follows. Bacon in any quantity about 12 hams, Dried apples. Beans of Flour (about enough till Salt Lake City.) Corn Meal plenty of Pilot Bread [*a hard, long-lasting biscuit]*. Coffee. Tea. Sugar Salt, Rice & Pepper.

P. H. Elsworth the owner & proprietor of the train was an American and had been to California once before across the plains.[2] He had a tyranical disposition as the sequel will Show. He advertised in the press 3 months before departing that the train was in readiness at any time. The price for passage fixed by him was $100.00 per person through to California, He R^{eceiv}ed this money from 75 persons about six weeks before starting, $^{\&\ then\ he}$ hastily collected his train and thus established himself without Capital. But to proceed, There were 8 families in the train, there were about 75 persons as stated out of which there were about 10 Ladies, 5 boys and girls and the rest ~~was~~^{ere} men. The wagons were of a rather small size, and were each covered with an awning.

Turn Over [*note at the end of the first page*]

Monday April 26th 1852

We departed from Saint Louis Mo at about 11 oclock A. M. All went on very well till we had gained about 4 miles when the Tongue of Wagon No 7 broke which obliged us to lay by at "the Star" Tavern & "Bellevue" till next morning. The Cattle went along at a fine rate. At about 5 P.M. Fires were kindled, coffee made and we for the first time had a real taste of Life on the plains. Just about 8 oclock as we had tumbled into bed, it commenced to rain and continued until after 10 P.M. Came about 4 miles

Tuesday April 27th 1852

We had a hard time catching and yoking up the Cattle they being rather wild. We finally got ready and started from camp at 8 1-2 oclock. Nothing of interest occurred today. Camped at 5 oclock. Came 16 miles

Wednesday April 28th 1852

Started at about 7 oclock after going 1 mile discovered that the Coupling pole of Wagon No 5 was broken. Had to wait about an hour to repair and again Started. At 11 oclock passed "Manchester" a small place, and went on and arrived to Camp at about 5 1-2 oclock without further accident. Came about 17 miles

Thursday April 29th 1852

Started at 1-2 past 7 and camped at 1-2-past 2 P.M. Father went out hunting and killed some good Game. Nothing of interest occurred today. came 12 miles

P. S. We had an election for Captain today & Mr Scott was Elected

Friday April 30th 1852

Started at 7 oclock at about 10 oclock the axletree of wagon no "5" broke at three miles from the town of Union. After leaving "5ves" [*"fives"—the fifth wagon in the train*] to come in the rear, about ½ mile one of the Yokes of Wagon No 9 broke, No 4 all right. Camped in sight of Union at 5. Came 10 miles

P.S. At 8 No 5 came in on three wheels~

Saturday May 1st 1852

Started at 7 1-2 oclock. Bought tar at 5 cts per Lb. Passed Union at 8 A.M. This is a very nice place camped at 4 oclock. Came 14 miles

P.S. We left Captain Scott at Union very sick. He was a passenger and he had been unanimously elected captain of the Train. D. V. [*Dominique's initials*]

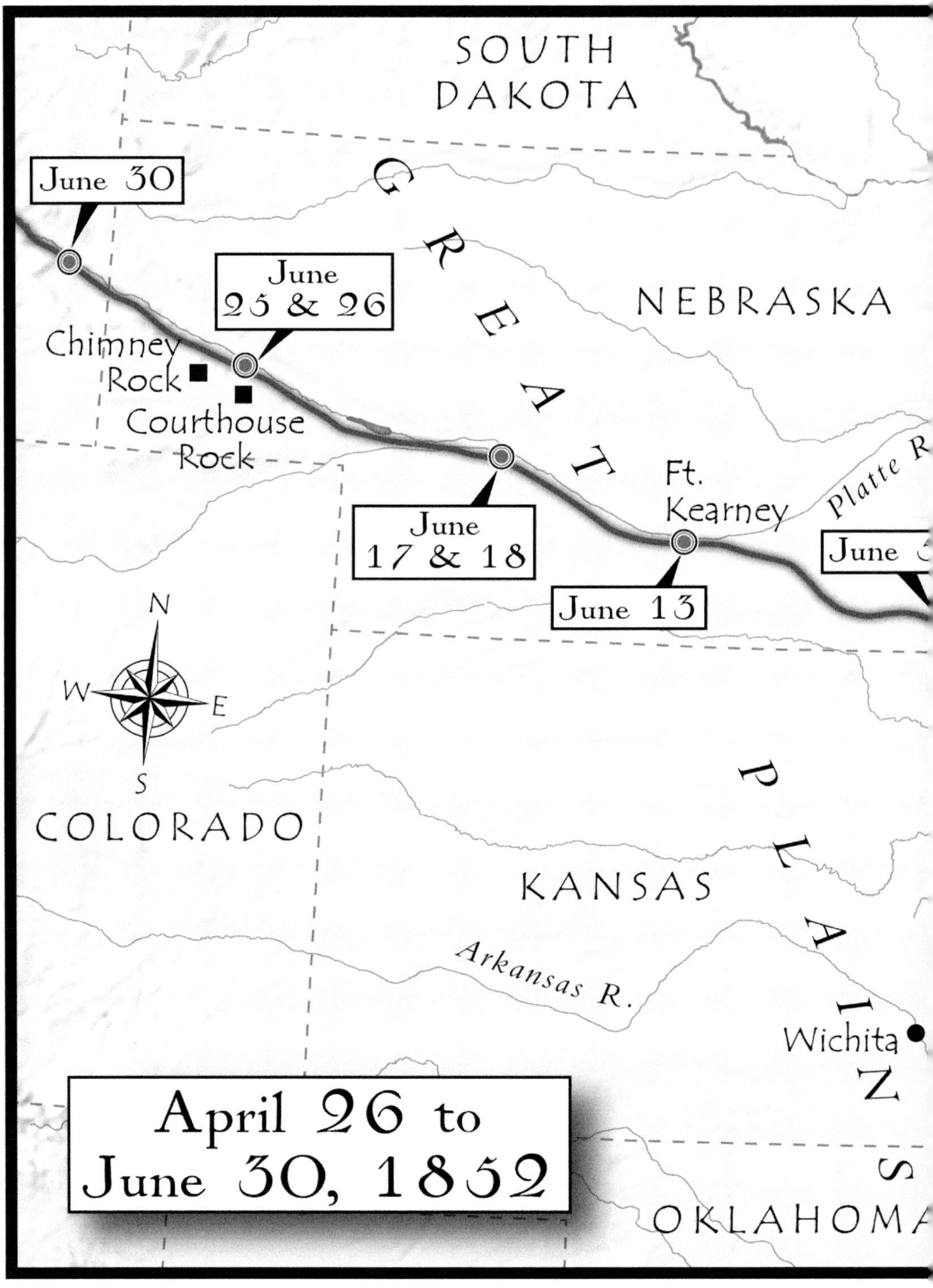
SOUTH DAKOTA
GREAT PLAINS
NEBRASKA
June 30
June 25 & 26
Chimney Rock
Courthouse Rock
June 17 & 18
Ft. Kearney
Platte R
June 13
N
W
E
S
COLORADO
KANSAS
Arkansas R.
Wichita
OKLAHOMA
April 26 to June 30, 1852

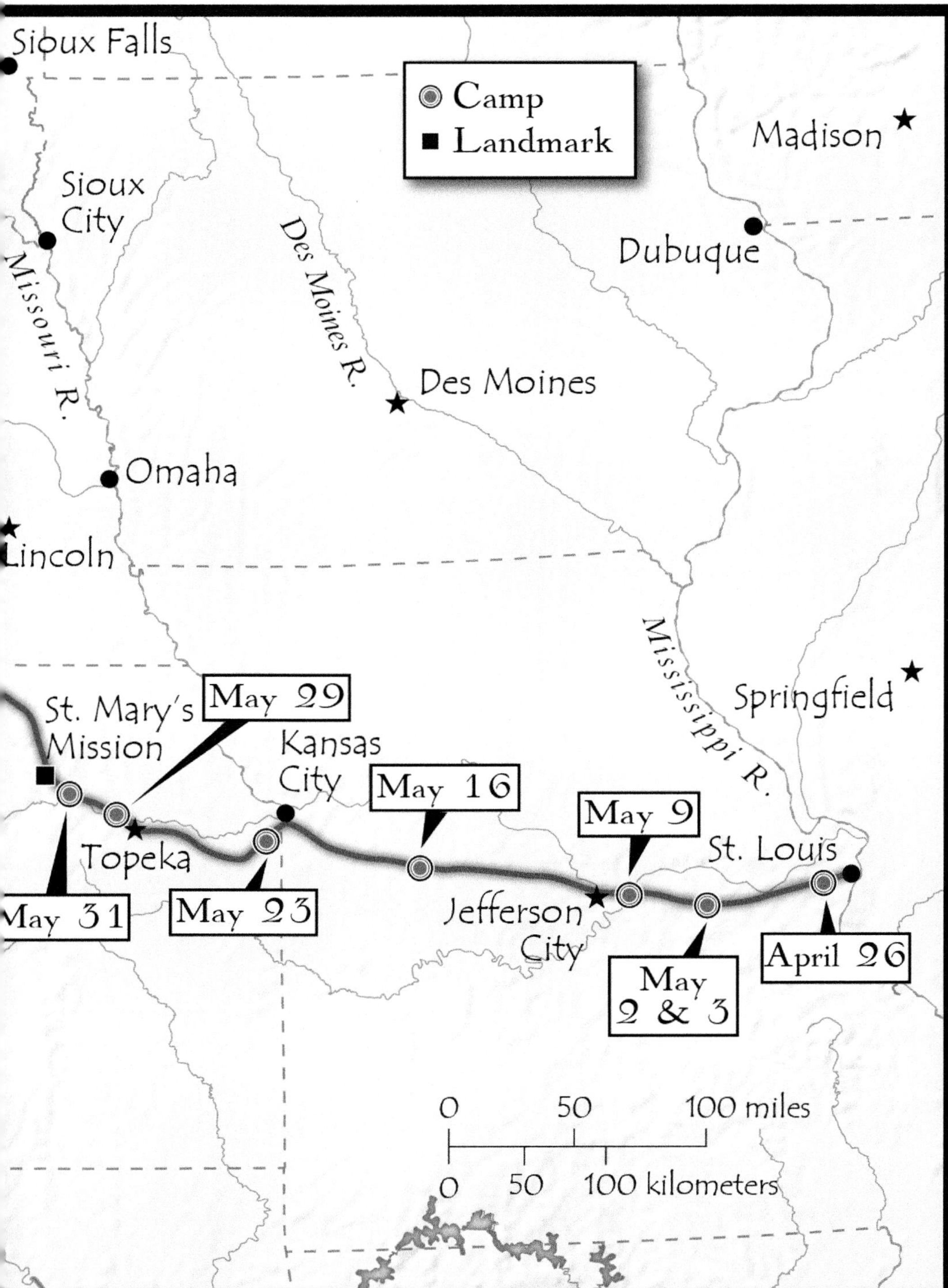

[Marin History Museum/Mary Rostad]

Sunday May 2nd 1852

Rolled out at 7 oclock. Camped at four oclock. At about 4 1-2 oclock, we were visited by a terrific storm accompanied by Hail, Rain, Thunder & Lightning. After it abated some, Father went out hunting and killed some nice squirrels & rabbits, but it was hard to cook them on acct of the rain (which had recommenced) it continued all night as hard as thunder. Came 13 miles

Monday May 3^{d} 1852

It is still raining which obliged us to lay by all day.
N.B.[3] Another reason is the creeks ahead are so swollen as not to be fordable

Tuesday May 4th 1852

Started at 7 oclock up a high rocky road, had to cut a road through the bushes. Had a very rough road today. Camped at four oclock at 1 ½ miles from the Gasconade River. Came 15 miles

Wednesday May 5th 1852

Started at 8 A.M. At 9 arrived at the Gasconade River. This river is about ⅓ of a mile wide and in some places very deep. On the left-hand side of the river are the ruins of a small town which was abandoned a few days before we arrived it was said on account of the "Black Vomit" [*yellow fever*]. We ferried the river on a small scow large enough to hold 1 wagon conveniently. We crossed without any accident. The loose cattle swam the river but with an ill grace. Camped at 4. Came 7 miles
Note The manner in which the scow was rowed from one side to the other is as follows: a Line was stretched clear Across the river and 2 men (one at each end) would then pull it along while a 3^{d} would steer. It rained all night

Thursday May 6th '52

Started at ½ past 6 still raining. About 11 stopped to feed the Cattle. The mud is knee deep. Our Wagon No 4 had its tongue broke. Camped at four oclock in a very bad place on acct of the rain. Came 4 miles

Friday May 7th

Started at 7 o. Travelled this day through mud knee deep, and camped at Loose creek, where we received the sad intelligence that capt Scott had died, he left three children, to mourn his loss, in respect to his memory unanimous resolutions were passed that we deeply regretted and felt his loss etc~ this day came 11 miles.

Ferry Crossing the Kansas River
[*Kansas State Historical Society*]

Sunday May 8th

Started very early in the morning, proceeded five miles when we reached the Osage river, here we ferried over the wagons in a scow, and we attempted to make the oxen swim, across. Some half of a dozen accomplished this feat but the balance we had to ferry over. This retarded us for the balance of the day. We camped on the opposite shore where Mr Voteau's train of five wagons was awaiting us, to accompany our train, we were now in company Eighteen wagons

Sunday May 9th

Started at 1/2 past 6, travelled through a very hilly road, this day & frequently were stuck in a mud hole. Travelled on to the Mauro River [*Moreau River, Cole County, Missouri*], which we forded easily and camped on the opposite side for the night. Travelled this day 6 miles

Monday 10th

Started at 7 oclock and at noon arrived at Jefferson city, the Capital of the State of Missouri. Stopped the balance of the day at the city. We visited the State house, a fine building where the legislature meets. We also visited the state penitentiary, where we seen prisoners, of all hues from the pickpocket to the vilest murderer. This prison is surrounded by high walls of stone, every prisoner labours, and all kinds of articles are manufactured here. The city, owing to its high & hilly position, has made but little progress. Came this day 4 miles

Jefferson City, Missouri (1860s)
[*Library of Congress*]

Tuesday 11th

Laid by all day at the city. We shipped our provisions to Kansas on the steamboat Alton, this was necessary, because the mud was too deep ahead of us for our wagons to carry, 1 ton weight apiece.

Wednesday 12th

Departed from Jefferson city. Passed a single wagon bound for salt lake, camped a mile in the forest, the reason of this was to, feed the cattle, this being the nearest place where corn was to be had. Arrived 12 miles

Thursday 13

Laid by all day in the forest to recruit the then weak and fatigued cattle.[4]

Friday 14th

Went on and ferried the Bear river and camped at six where one of the most appalling circumstances occurred to us, It commenced to storm rain Thunder & lightning in the worst degree. It then commenced hailing in a way inconceivable only to the spectator. The hail fell so suddenly that I had no time to ensconce myself in the wagon for shelter, I therefore crept under the wagon. It continued unabated for two long hours during which time the cattle and horses dived in the neighboring forest. After it stopped hailing we in the obscurity preceded forth, we found some of the hailstones to be the size of a large hen egg, we were all drenched through. In fact we were in a dismal plight for that night. Our horses & cattle gone, no one knew where, and we cold and wet, came this day 14 miles. This Friday proved unlucky

"Storm on the Prairie"

[*Overland in 1846: Diaries and Letters of the California-Oregon Trail, Dale Morgan, University of Nebraska Press, 1993*]

Saturday 15th

Laid by all day. We found many birds rabbits fishes and other animals that had been killed by the hail. The cattle were all found again today. The grass was all cut by the hail

Sunday 16th

Started at six and camped at four oclock. This was the finest day for traveling we have had yet as we came 26 miles~~~~~

P. S The road was very level and no dust.

Monday 17th

Rolled out at 7 oclock and at about 11 oclock passed the small town of Warrenburg [*Warrensburg, county seat of Johnson County, Missouri*]. Camped at four and a half oclock. Came 17 miles. Warrenburg contains about 500 inhabitants and has about 120 houses. It contains several Hotels and Groceries Stores and a few other Shops~~~~~

Tuesday 18th

We were rather late getting off today, the horses and Cattle having Strayed about 2 miles from camp. We started at 9 and at about noon forded the Black Water Creek. It derives it name from the fact that the water is rather black & brackish. Camped at ½ past Eight oclock. Had a very good road. Came 26 miles

Wednesday 19th

Started at six and camped at 5 oclock. Came 15 miles. In the evening killed a Calf which was divided into 16 messes.

Thursday 20th

Started from camp at 1/2 past six oclock. During the day we forded the little blue river, in fording we were obliged to raise the wagon beds 1 foot ~~and~~ the river had a very strong current. I was also thrown from my horse a rather wild and prancing pony, I sustained no bodily injury, but the saddle did, it was completely shattered. This day came 17 miles, and we're now within 6 miles of Kansas, the city to which we had shipped our provisions

Friday 21st

Laid by all day, in the morning Nine wagons were dispatched to Kansas, to receive our provisions, in returning, No 8 ran against a stump, and careened over, in which evolution a keg of tar which the vehicle contained was bespattered against its sides and ever after bore the mark of the tar of Kansas, our provisions arrived to camp in good order and were then equally repacked in our wagons.

Saturday 22nd

Continued still to lay by, during which time we proceeded to elect a captain, Mr Bulloc of No 10 was one of the candidates, the other was Lieutenant Cohen, No 3. The first mentioned gentlemen received the unanimous vote of the company and was therefore duly elected

Sunday 23rd

Departed from camp at 1/2 past 7, It was now that we were going to cross the plains, the traveling we had done before, was through the state, we now passed the dividing line of the State of Missouri and the Indian Territory. We then bid adieu to Missouri once oxen harnessed.

Came 16 miles

Monday 24th

Started at 7 on a level and fair road. Camped at 12 on account of the heavy fall of rain. Came 10 miles. A rolling prairie interspersed with fine grass and flowers was the country around

Tuesday 25th

Left camp at 6 oclock, proceeded onwards, & had to ford a narrow river whose banks were exceedingly steep and muddy. Wagon No 8, the unlucky tar wagon, in descending the bank [precipated] Mrs. James, an Irish lady, in the river. She was quickly rescued to the mirth of some and the seriousness of others. Travelled this day 25 miles

Wednesday 26th

Laid by all day, killed five Rattle snakes. We also beheld a large rock on which we found many names cut in the rock. We also added ours~~~~~

Thursday 27th

Started at 1/2 past six. At 8 arrived at [Wokalouchuh] creek [*Wakarusa River near Lawrence, Kansas*] which detained us till noon, in crossing and then in the afternoon made 18 miles, in all 25 miles. Same day passed Kentucky train of Hobbs & Co which consisted of 18 wagons, to day went through a forest.

Friday 28th

Started at 6, went at good rate, having a fine road to travel on. The yoke of one of the oxen of wagon No 9 broke, which detained us. We camped two miles off the road to find grass for the cattle. Came this day 24 miles[5]

Saturday 29th

Started at 6, went on and arrived at the Kansas or Kaw [*still an alternative name for the Kansas River*] River, which we forded. I and many others of the train bathed in this river, during the day we met, one wagon returning from its intended voyage viz [*namely*] to California. The wagon consisted of two men, both brothers, one of whom lost his wife ahead, leaving him & his brother to take care of 6 children, 1 not more than 12 months old. Under this burden with the news he had learned he thought the wiser plan was to return to the states. The news he spoke of was that, ahead of us, the Cholera & smallpox was raging, in unbated fury, and that many of the emigrants were returning. This intelligence although bad did not discourage us and so we travelled on and put our trust in Providence, travelled this day 24 miles. Father bought a pacing [*faster than a trot, slower than a gallop*] mare for Dominick for the small sum of 30 dollars.

Sunday 30th

Started at nine, nothing of interest worth mentioning occurred this day. Came twenty three miles

Monday the 31st

Started at 6 oclock, at nine arrived at an Indian village called St. Mary's Mission,[6] it was principaly occupied by civilised indians who farmed their lands, having something to repair, we stopped there until it was done. Departed and camped at six, came this day 22 miles, there are probaly about 40 houses in this settlement.

St. Mary's Mission
[*Kansas State Historical Society*]

Tuesday June 1st

Started at 6, Forded the Vermilion river [*a tributary of the Kansas River, west of Belvue, Kansas*], came this day 24 miles. Several of the men during the day went out hunting, they succeeded in killing a fine deer, which was equally divided among 13 messes. We found it to be very good and quite exceptable after eating the salt Bacon pilot bread & beans. The Country around here is very fine abounding in prairies

Wednesday the 2nd

Started at 6, came to camp at 7 oclock. Several of the loose cattle ran away which caused much trouble among the drivers. They had to go back & chase the cattle about 10 miles before they succeeded in capturing them. Came 26 miles

Thursday 3rd

Started at six. At noon number 13 had its tongue broke. We met a large train of 21 wagons returning on account of sickness, crossed the big blue river,[7] and camped 1 mile off the road, the reason we camped so far from the road was that emigrant's stock which had passed near the road ahead, of us had eaten all the grass, which caused us to camp far from the road. We amused ourselves this day in fishing. The water of the river was as clear as crystal. Came 25 miles

Pioneer Covered Wagon River Crossing, 1870

[©iStock.com/bauhaus1000]

Friday 4th

Decamped at six. This day we followed up the blue river.[8] The country around is beautiful abounding in undulated plains covered with grass. Met several wagons this day. Came 25 miles

Saturday 5th

Started at 7. This day we had a good joke. Several men of our train went out hunting. They found a lame ox in the woods which they slaughtered. They said they had killed a Buffalo, they brought some of the beef with them to camp. They waved it in triumph, and said they had had the honor, to kill the first buffalo, the matter soon blew up, one of them informing the company of the truthful story. We camped this day at nine P.M. 21 miles

Sunday 6th

Started at six, travelled about 11. Found that the coupling pole of No 7 was broken. We therefore halted and met a company of Rocky mountain mountaineers. They were returning to the states with heavy wagons loaded with furs of different animals principally of Buffalo & deer skins. Travelled until night when we camped again on the borders of the blue. Came 22 miles.

Monday 7th

departed very early from camp, this day we saw a very melancholy spectacle on the side of the road. three sisters buried in one grave, 1 aged 32 another 26 and the last 21. Their names and ages were carved on a plank placed at the head of their grave. Came 25 miles

Tuesday 8th

started at six, went on and saw many graves. At noon P. H. Elsworth who had gone on ahead, his usual occupation during the day, he came back pale as a sheet, stating that about five hundred Indians ahead were in ambuscade to attack us. at this intelligence each man seized his gun. Rifle. pistol, etc. determined to have a battle. At long last on the brow of the hill, we saw some forty Indians. They came on towards us without any hostile attempt. They were all armed & mounted. Each bore a rifle, Pistol. Knife tomahawk and lance. they gave us to understand that they were at war with an indian tribe called the Cheyennes [*The raiders were most likely Pawnees*]. They showed us which disgusted us some Scalps of the cheyennes. We gave them some victuals [*pronounced 'vittles," food or provisions*] and they departed leaving Elsworth to be jeered at, travelled until night and camped. Came twenty seven miles. We now for the first time beheld the mountains of the Platte river in the distance. Came 23 miles

Wednesday 9th

started at 6, camped at 3, came 15 Miles.

P.S. since we left Kansas the weather has continued fine and dry with the exception of the dust

Thursday 10th

started very early having to travel Twenty seven miles for water. the nearest being that of the Platte, travelled through a rough road and at about five P.M. reached the Platte, this river is very wide in some places 1½ miles wide. the water is muddy this is the reason the Mississippi river below its junction with the Missouri is so muddy. this river derives its name from the fact of its being shallow [*Rivière Plate, named by French trappers, means "flat river"*]. The banks also are very low, came this day 27 miles.

Camp of Pawnee on the Platte Valley (1866)
[*Library of Congress/John Carbutt*]

Friday 11

started about 9 oclock, went on till noon and camped again on the Platte which river we are destined to travel along its borders several hundred miles, near our camping ground we saw a grave enclosed with logs to prevent the wolves tearing up the ground which they often did. We were now within a mile and a half from fort Kearny,[9] came this day 10 miles.

Saturday 12th

laid by all day, as we were near fort Kearny, we had plenty of grass. most of the men went to the river and washed their clothes, while others went hunting & to Fort Kearny, it was a fine day, wood is very scarce had to hunt for buffalo chips, the manure of the Buffalo, when dry it burns well and is most as good as coal, by the help of it we baked our bread

Sunday 13th

Went on and arrived at fort Kearny, all kinds of provisions were sold here, at exorbitant prices, the officers of the fort were very courteous and invited us inside the fort, here we saw some forty american soldiers, they were about to start in pursuit of Indians, I believe the Pawnees, they brang two field pieces [*cannons on carriages*] with them, they were all mounted. the cause of their departure was that three men had complained at the fact that having one wagon with ten oxen they were attacked by the indians, which caused them to flee and all their stock fell into the hands of the Pawnees. passed several large trains among which was Lake's Tennessee train, and camped this night twenty two miles from fort Kearny, in all about twenty five miles. wood again very scarce, we resorted to Buffalo chips, It also rained this night

Fort Kearny, Nebraska (1864)
[*L. Tom Perry Special Collections, Harold B. Lee Library, Brigham Young University, Provo, Utah, MSS 1608, cropped*]

Monday 14th

Started at five, A.M., during this day we found many mushrooms, on the side, and off the road, we descended from our horses, and wagons, and gathered quantities; Elsworth said they were poisonous, there were some botanists in the train that knew better, we cooked and found them to taste exceedingly nice, at five P.M we met a party of mountaineers with heavy wagons transporting to the U.S the usual products of the rocky mountains, they presented us with some buffalo meat dried in the sun. we knew some of them in Saint. Louis; they were mostly Creoles & canadians, the wind blew strong this day. the mountaineers told us we would yet, see stronger gales, than this & so we afterwards did, came twenty eight miles.

Tuesday 15th

started at five, had some trouble to find the cattle this day, I and father went on ahead of the train to get some wood, we stopped long enough in the woods, to have the train ahead of us several miles, we had to go very slow on account of the wood we carried, although on horseback, we at length arrived at the train at night, we unloaded our wood and tied it behind the wagon, came twenty six miles this day.

Wednesday 16th

started at six, during the day one of the Cohen brothers was missing, he had been out early hunting not arriving at night, we kindled large bond-fires, and fired guns, in the hope that he would arrive, and he did arrive at two oclock in the morning, quite weakened, and fatigued. He said that during the day he lost his way, and fatigued his pony much in endeavoring, to go different paths, and night approaching he descended from his horse, seized the lariat and let the pony go on ahead, the pony followed in his former footsteps and he was soon again on the road. he walked 10 miles to find our camp which was the cause of his late arrival, he saw our fires and heard our guns which enabled him to find our camp, came 23 miles.

Thursday 17th

Started at five, during the day the weather was fine, I and many others took a race, I came off second best but my horse stumbled and I fell over his neck. I was not injured neither was my horse, came twenty four miles, killed an antelope, which we divided as usual ~~came~~

Friday 18th

This day we laid by all day to see whether the south fork of the platte was fordable, during the day many of the cattle got astray, they were recovered, with the loss of an ox, which we could not find.

Saturday 19th

Went on and reached the south fork of the Platte, here we saw about ~~a~~ 1 hundred wagons, engaged in crossing. the river here was about half a mile wide, succeeded in crossing it in safety, we forded, but had to raise the wagon beds, six inches; had much trouble to get the cattle across, they would cut through the river in every way, went on a few miles & camped, came 8 miles[10]

Sunday 20th

laid by all day on account of the sickness of Mrs Cody. weather very windy here, at a trading post ~~???d~~ cognac was selling at two dollars a pint, we did indulge in it

Crossing the Platte (1859)
[*Library of Congress/Albert Bierstadt*]

Monday 21st

Mrs Cody had got better, we started off, weather fine. Mr Davis in the morning, 1 of the passengers, purged himself [*severe diarrhea is a symptom of cholera*], in doing so he caught cold, we were now in the black mountains, and not finding grass, and being in a thick cold fog, we did not wait here, perhaps it would have been much better had we did, poor Mr Davis begged for the sake of God to stop. But Elsworth would not. we camped at 8 oclock in a place where there was plenty of water and grass. Mr Davis at 11 oclock in the night expired, he a wife in the train but no children, came 21 miles

Tuesday 22nd

The first thing in the morning we did was the solemn spectacle of interring Mr Davis, two men proceeded to dig a grave, which they quickly finished, it was six feet deep, two and a half feet wide, and six feet long, he was lowered enveloped in his blanket, and in a few minutes was in, that bourn [*From the French "bourne"—a goal or destination*], from which no traveler returns, a the head of his grave we placed a board which bore the following inscription,

John Davis
of St. Louis, Mo
died June 21st 1852
aged 52 of Choleral

and so the solemn and impressive spectacle ended, and again we travelled on for that land we seemed to never reach, "California." camped at four oclock, came 18 miles

Wednesday 23rd

started at six, taking a cutoff from the Platte, had to travel 29 miles before we again touched it, we accomplished this, but the cattle were dreadfully fatigued and at our camping ground saw many dead cattle, which had died from the alkali springs [*poisonous waters*], between the cutoff and the platte. It was with much trouble that we stopped our cattle from drinking this bad water. came 29 miles

Thursday 24th

High winds, started at 6, at 9 one of the wagons was upset, No 11 in running against a log, it was quickly righted with little injury. I was also thrown from my horse in carrying wood. I was as usual uninjured. I landed with the wood on the ground, came 25 miles

Friday 25th

Started at six, passed a train of fourteen wagons, from Indiana another of four, and about 1 hour afterwards saw a train of Five thousand sheep, bound for California, we stopped at two oclock, some of these men visited, Court house rock,[11] it was 12 miles off the road, and did not seem more than two; It a curiosity of nature and is is similar to a large court house, it is of sandstone, came 18 miles

Saturday 26th

laid by all day on account of sickness, two men of No 7 being sick, we were in sight of Chimney rock,[12] another of nature's freaks, the men washed their clothes this day in the Platte, while others bathed, we could now plainly distinguish Laramie Peak [*113 miles northwest of Chimney Rock, Wyoming*], it appeared like a large cloud in the distance

Sunday 27th

started at five, travelled fast four miles from Chimney rock, we visited this rock, from its base to its top it is four hundred and forty eight feet high, innumerable names are cut on it, I should not doubt 100,000, the rock ascends from its base in the shape of an inclined plane and then the chimney about forty feet high ascends, passed the chimney & camped, ~~came~~ came twenty two miles

Chimney Rock
[*History Nebraska/Image RG3319-03-01*]

Monday 28th

went on and soon arrived at Scotts bluffs [*Scottsbluff, Nebraska*]. They are nearly perpendicular, and at the point where we were we could not reach the top, had to pass through a rocky canõn barely wide enough to enable the wagons to pass [*probably Robidoux Pass*], we passed it was soon on a nice & smooth, road and stopped for a while at a trading post, went on & came 25 miles.

Tuesday 29th

Laid by all day on account of the sickness of Mr Lyles

Wednesday 30th

started at six, weather fine, during the day hailed the; returning from california train; they said california was not worth anything; men were hired at $50 per month etc, camped 16 miles, from fort Laramie, came twenty seven miles, the weather was fine, here at a trading post flour was worth 20 cts a pound.[13] Soap 50 cts a bar, sugar sugar 60 cts per pound, and other provisions in the same ratio. here Elsworth exchanged several horses and cattle, he also got 2 of his horses shod for which he paid 16 dollars, horse shoe nails sold for $1 a dozen, horses were cheap, their price not exceeding $50

Scott's Bluff Visitor's Center
[*Library of Congress*]

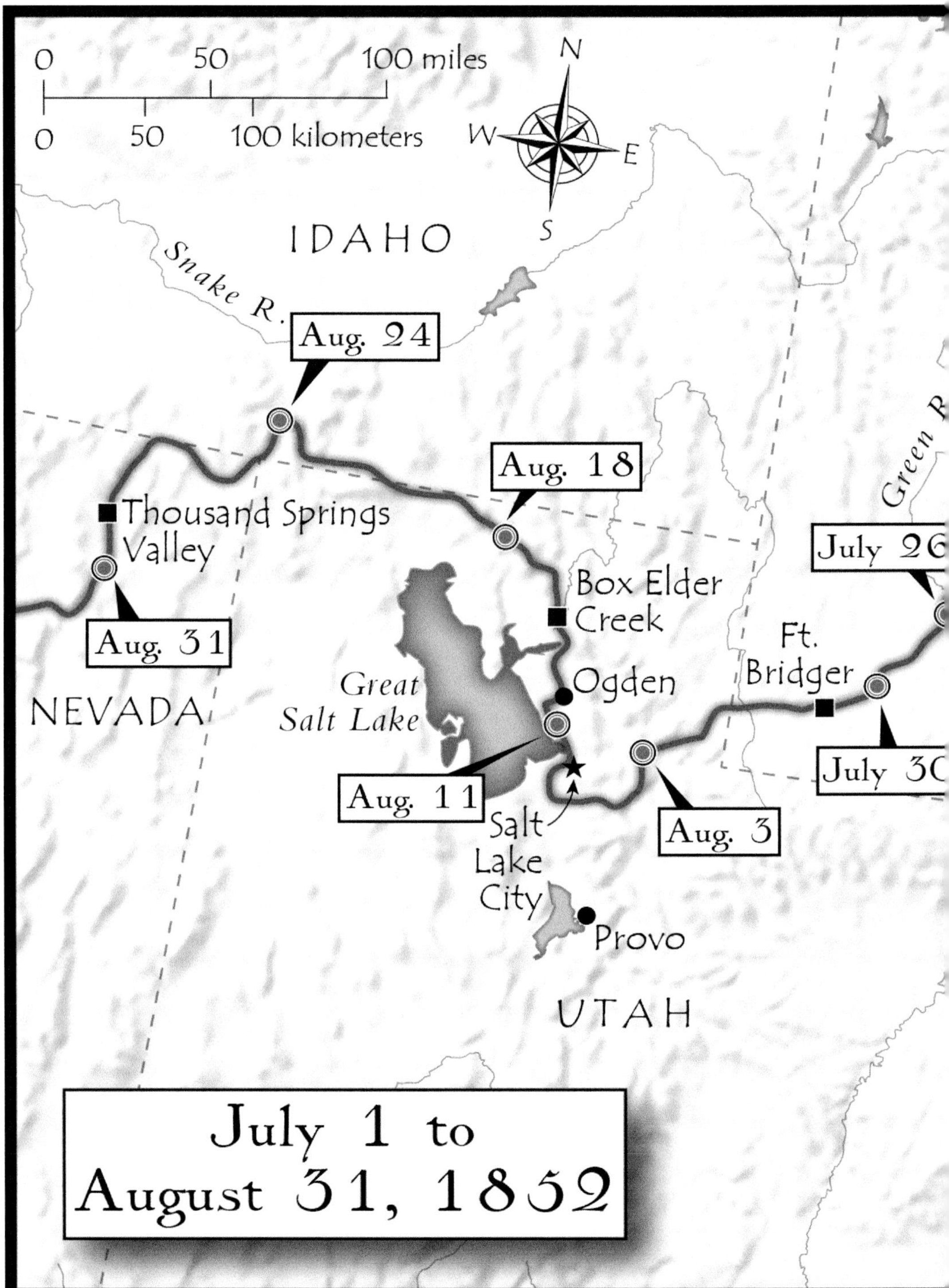
0 50 100 miles
0 50 100 kilometers
N
W
E
S
IDAHO
Snake R.
Aug. 24
Aug. 18
Thousand Springs Valley
Aug. 31
NEVADA
Green R.
July 26
Box Elder Creek
Ft. Bridger
Ogden
Great Salt Lake
Aug. 11
Aug. 3
July 30
Salt Lake City
Provo
UTAH
July 1 to August 31, 1852

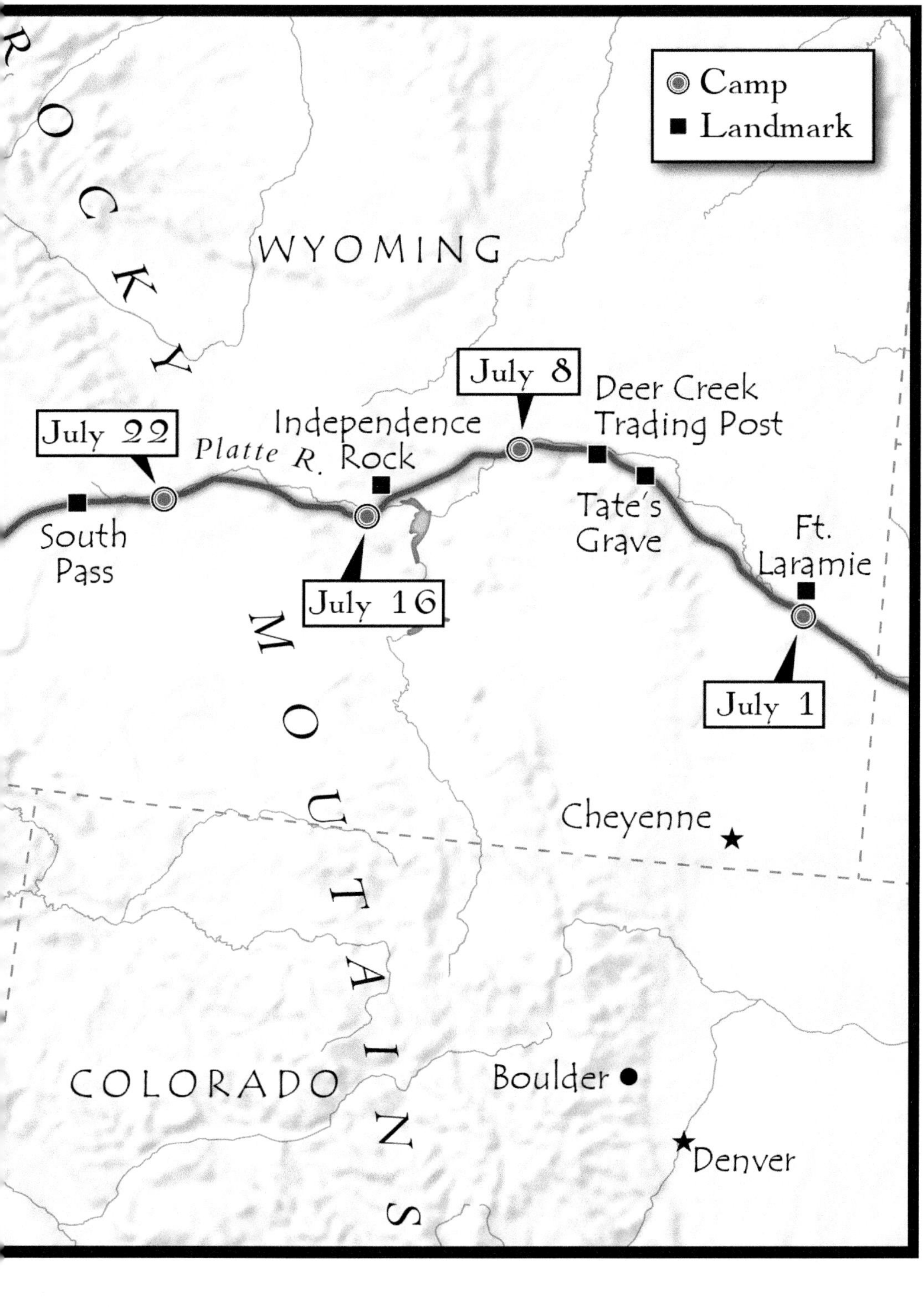

[Marin History Museum/Mary Rostad]

Fort Laramie (1855)
[L. Tom Perry Special Collections, Harold B. Lee Library, Brigham Young University, Provo, Utah, MSS 273.41]

Thursday July 1st

started at six. met several handcarts, 3, if I mistake not, each having 8 men, four to pull in the morning, while the others walked by the side and they in return in the afternoon drew while the others walked. each handcart carried in weight including baggage & provisions Six hundred pounds. they offered to beat us on to california, which we did not take, they did not like us; wait for grass for cattle; went on & came to a trading post opposite Laramie River on the opposite shore was fort Laramie. Elsworth paid two dollars a wagon, to cross on the bridge & 10 ^{cts} per head for cattle & horses.[14] we were now about Eleven hundred miles from St Louis. M$^{o.}$ we camped about a mile and a half below Fort Laramie, the fort is poorly built. the front is a three story frame house and a large yard enclosed with adobe walls. there are also many small adobe houses in its vicinity being populated mostly by Indians and mountaineers. came 20 miles, here again we met some mountaineers who informed us that we were now within Six hundred miles of Salt Lake city, and that we yet had the worst road to travel.

Friday July 2nd

left the neighborhood of Fort Laramie early in the morning at about four oclock. laramie peak was on our left hand side, its top was capped with snow. It was eighteen miles off the road and therefore we did not visit it. camped in the afternoon again on the borders of the Platte [*near Guernsey, Wyoming*]. grass scarce. we were assailed during the night by hosts of Mosquitoes. this caused the horses and cattle to kick wildly. Came 18 Miles

Saturday July 3rd

Started at six. weather fine. camped on a high eminence, plenty of water and grass. our company in high spirits, we made a big fire this night to salute the eve of 4th of July. came 18 miles

Sunday July 4th

started a six along a fine road. camped one mile off the road on the banks of a beautiful brook, in this camping ground we found many yokes chains etc to numerous to mention. in the night we erected a tremendous fire and Mr Dolittle and several others made speeches. most of the company remained up till two oclock. some singing to the tune of a Violin, they were in high glee and long will I remember this night. came & made 14 miles

Monday July 5th

Started at six. many of the loose cattle astray, the drivers were therefore obliged to wait their recovery. during the day saw the grave of T. Miller, died June 10th 1852. he was murdered in cold blood by a man named Lafayette Tate. camped, when the cattle that had been astray in the morning arrived, wether cool & pleasant

Tuesday July 6th

started early. crossed Bosame Creek where I gleaned the following particulars of the murderer Tate.[15] It appeared that Tate had informed some one in Miller's train that as soon as he would be out of Reach of Fort Laramie, he would kill miller. and he (miller) going on one day ahead of the train, Tate stabbed him to the heart [*see Endnotes for more on Tate and the murder*].[16] Tate was immediately brought before a tribunal, representatives from 200 wagons in the neighborhood. Tate had a fair and impartial trial. by them, he was sentenced to be hung and his remains buried but 1 foot below the sod so that his body would become the prey of wolves & other animals. This sentence was fully carried into effect and thus Tate paid the deep penalty for his crime. when we passed near this day, we noticed his grave from which one of his bones protruded forth and his hair was strewed around the grave. It was a shocking sight.

During the day we also killed 2 fine antelopes. came 18 miles. camped at four P.M.

Tate was but 19 years of age and it was said that he had wealthy and respectable parents in the states. he had a brother who the immigrants attempted to hang for this reason. Tate, before arriving in Fort Laramie, told his brother that before long he would murder Miller. He [*Tate's brother*] confessed this after the bloody deed was done. for not confessing before they tried to Lynch him. they had gone as far as to put the rope around his neck, when a party of immigrants rushed to his rescue. And one making a hearty appeal in his behalf, he was quickly liberated. they gave him a horse. with it he galloped forward and was never heard of after

Wednesday July 7th

started at six. during the day killed a buffalo. had a rough road. were now about to enter the black hills. camped in a place where we found many gooseberries and a trading post [*later the Deer Creek Pony Express Station at Glenrock, Wyoming*] where Elsworth exchanged some of his cattle. came 25 miles

Thursday July 8th

Started at seven. weather fine but windy. camped at six. made 18 miles. we again struck the north fork of the Platte. came 18 miles

Friday July 9th

Started at six. Went three miles when we camped, came 3 miles, wood scarce. ~~came 3 miles~~

Saturday July 10th

Started at seven. weather hot. dust in quantities, the drivers were obliged to wear goggles to prevent the dust entering their eyes, during the day Ira Hight, Denis Sawyer said they killed 2 buffaloes. Elsworth betted twenty dollars they had not, the bet was accepted and Hight & Sawyer accompanied by Elsworth's brother law started off to show the remains of the Buffaloes. came 20 miles

Sunday July 11th

started at six. Haight, Sawyer & David Mun returned to camp without finding the Buffaloe. Hight & Sawyer therefore lost the bet. came ferried the north fork of Platte river and camped one mile on the other side. price to cross the river $three per wagon. there were several trading posts on the borders of the river. came & made 4 miles.

Monday July 12th

started at six. weather pleasant but road very rough and rocky. came into a fine valley which we soon left and camped. came eighteen miles

Tuesday July 13th

left camp early. we were now in sight of Wind river and Rocky Mts. Nothing of occurrence happened this day, we travelled as usual. wood scarce in camp, I had to go one miles and a half a foot to get some wood among the mountains. came during this day. we bid adieu to the Platte river [*they had followed the Platte River for 500 miles*]. came 16 good miles

Wednesday July 14th

Started at six. travelled along an even road passing a trading post near which we camped and laid by the balance of the day. Independence rock perceptible in the distance. came ten miles.

Thursday July 15th

decamped at 7. struck the Sweet water river and there laid by all day. this river is not over ten yards wide and not more than two feet deep. here to lighten the wagons we made them shorter by cutting the wagon beds. during the day killed two Antelopes, grass in abundance, wood scarce. we were two miles off the road, in our vicinity was a large spring whose water, as clear as crystal, was cool and good, this we preferred to the sweet water river

"Along the Sweetwater River"

[*Overland in 1846: Diaries and Letters of the California-Oregon Trail, Dale Morgan, University of Nebraska Press, 1993*]

Friday July 16th

started at six. camped near the Devils gate. also passed independence rock,[17] this rock is composed of solid granite, it was not over 60 feet high but many times longer. here we saw thousands of names of immigrants who passed as far as the year 1846, two of the names I recognized, they were all painted black. The Devils gate is more of a curiosity, it is a large opening between two perpendicular rocks, 400 feet high each.[18] between these rocks, the Sweet Water river passes

Independence Rock (1870)
[*National Archive and Records Administration/William Henry Jackson*]

Independence Rock Signatures – R. McCord 1850
[*Goretexguy/CC BY-SA creativecommons.org/licenses/by-sa/4.0*]

Devil's Gate (1870)
[*National Archive and Records Administration/William Henry Jackson*]

Saturday July 17th

this day left camp at 7 and during the day had a very rough & rocky road. camped at 8 oclock. made 24 miles

Sunday July 18th

Started at six. weather hot, soon had a cold rain about 11 oclock. our wagon N° 4 in descending the bank of the river careened over. I was in it but was not hurt. It was righted in an instant and we again pursued our way. camped at three. came 14 miles

Monday July 19th

started at 7. weather pleasant, had a very hilly road to travel, we were now following one of the ridges of the Rocky mountains. came came 18 miles.

Tuesday July 20th

Started at 7 and camped at 10 A.M where grass was knee high. there were many antelopes in the vicinity as also snakes, here we shot the fattest beef we had which was equally divided among 13 Messes. came 4 Miles

Wednesday July 21st

laid by all day. father killed four sage hens and the balance of the company in proportion. laid by on the banks of a small creek where we caught some fish

Greater Sage Grouse
[*Bureau of Land Management*]

Thursday July 22nd

laid by all morning. started from camp at two oclock and in the evening camped on Strawberry creek

Friday July 23rd

started at six. about two reached the south Pass of the rocky mountains, it is eighteen miles wide and as even as a floor, in it was the Pacific springs, a fine spring, the water like ice, this the rocky mountains is the dividing side of the Atlantic & Pacific oceans. during the time we were here some of the Cattle went into a deep marsh and were with considerable difficulty extricated. went on & camped at Pacific creek. came 15 miles. This morning Mr. Voteau's train left us and went on

Saturday July 24th

Started at six. we had now a sandy road, no grass & in its stead the wild sage plant, only good for burning. Elsworth said that having heard there was plenty of grass water & provisions by the Salt lake route. he would go that way as also by this we evaded a desert of fifty five miles long [*fifteen miles northeast of Farson, Wyoming*].[19] came 15 miles. camped again on Pacific creek

Sunday July 25th

started at six. road sandy & dusty, had to go 25 miles before we could have water. I and several others on horse back went on ahead of the train and although we drove our horses hard, they did not seem to make any headway but at last we arrived at big Sandy creek. in the middle of the creek was an island with trees on it, there we waited till six oclock when the train came up, came twenty five miles. Grass this night scarce

Monday July 26th

started at six. forded the Big sandy and again during the day had a dusty road & camped eight miles from green river, we drove our cattle far below us in the valley, covered with grass where they regaled themselves, they much needed it, came 14 miles

Tuesday July 27th

started at six. at about 11 we reached the green river a large and clear stream of good water travelled along it southerly for about three miles where we camped, we caught many fish, in the river, here we had plenty of wood, the river is lined with it. Elsworth had a quarrel with one of the Passengers, he went as far as to produce his revolver. it was afterward settled without much difficulty. came 8 miles

Wednesday July 28th

Forded Green river. this we did by raising the wagon beds some 6 inches, we arrived in safety on the opposite shore, at the same time two men of our train left us, they were hungarians, we had known them in St Louis, they packed their provisions on 2 horses while they rode on the other two, Elsworth did not reimburse them anything, we travelled along the green river & camped at 12. laid by the balance of the day. came 7 miles, here was a large trading post kept by persons we knew in Saint. Louis; they sent our family some fresh provisions quite exceptable after the fatigue we had experienced the last few days. Flour was selling at 20 cts a pound. sugar 15 cts. Bacon 50 cts. coffee 1.00. Soap 75 cts a bar, tobacco and sigars were enormously high. came five miles

Thursday July 29th

started at six. road fair & water in plenty, and a little too much, had to pass many small muddy creeks, the banks nearly perpendicular; this caused us much delay. camped at 6. came 16 miles

Friday July 30th

started at six. forded hams forks [*named for Zacharias Hamm; northwest of Granger, Wyoming*] a small creek 15 feet wide and two feet deep. came 17 miles

Saturday 31st

Started at six. passed several shallow streams during the day & arrived at Fort Brider, one hundred and twelve miles from Salt Lake city, the fort is comprised of three log houses, we saw Bridger the old mountaineer [*see End Notes for Bridger's biography*].[20] he inhabited this place for 30 yrs. came 20 miles. camped at the fort, grass in abundance

Fort Bridger (1852)
[*The Miriam and Ira D. Wallach Division of Art, Prints and Photographs: Print Collection, The New York Public Library. (1852). Fort Bridger, Black's Fork of Green River. Retrieved from http://digitalcollections.nypl.org/items/510d47d9-7ccd-a3d9-e040-e00a18064a99*]

Sunday August 1st

Started at six from Fort Bridger travelled on a very even road, travelled through the snake indian tribe, camped on a clear brook, grass in plenty.[21] came 22 miles

Monday 2nd August

started at six & struck the bear river mountains [*probably near Evanston, Wyoming*], met the mail from Salt lake returning to the United States, the carriers told us to beware, indians were ahead etc, struck bear river a fine stream thirty feet wide by 2 ½ feet deep. Its bottom was of cobble stones. caught some trout in the river, went on & camped at six, made 22 miles. camped on snake creek, a narrow but deep stream of water, weather very pleasant.

Tuesday 3rd

started at six, road commenced to be rather mountainous, N° 10 broke its coupling pole, camped at David's spring [*near Emory, Utah*]. Came 20 miles,

Wednesday 4th

forded weber river in the morning a stream similar to the bear river and crossed several other streams some very muddy, we were now fairly in the mountains. camped near a trading post thirty miles from Salt lake. Potatoes here $2.00 a bushel, came 18 miles

Thursday 5th

travelled on through a canyon road very rocky, commenced to ascend the great mountain, which was done with much dificulty as well as the fatigue of the cattle, descended with more ease and camped aside of a blacksmith shop 13 miles from Salt lake city [*near South Weber, Utah*], we had plenty of grass. Came 20 miles

Friday 6th

laid by all day, got some cattle shod, many left temporarily to visit S. L. city

Saturday 7th

continued to lay by, got the tires of the wagon cut and horses and cattle shod

Sunday 8th

some cattle were exchanged and others shod, were getting tired of stopping, learned that Voteau was ahead of us 2 weeks

Monday 9th

left our old camping ground at six, went on and soon were in sight of the city of the great salt lake, at two oclock we reached it, the city is squarely built, the streets are very broad, and run at right angles, the houses present a neat appearance, they are mostly built of adobe, and then painted white, each block in the city in the average does not contain more than three houses; the balance is all farmed, and used to raise animals, such as Cattle. Poultry etc, one of the finest buildings is Brigham Young's the governor's residence, the state house is also a fine edifice.

The city is watered from one end to the other by ditches, being dug from a fine stream near the city, this water is very pure & clear and there being no hills in the city, it was brought with considerable ease, there are also some fine stores in the city, one occupied by Holladay & Warner for fancy goods, we, I mean Elsworth, bought 1000 lbs. of Flour for the train, about 80 pounds for each wagon; saw one of the mormon temples, the city is situated in a large valley in which the great salt lake lies embosomed; in the lake is a large mountain, and the whole valley around is surrounded by mountains, wood is scarce, and can only be got but from the mountains. the valley is covered with verdure, and the climate throughout is one of the finest in the world.

The authorities prohibit the use of liquors, and smoking or chewing tobacco, they also discountenance, swearing & profane language, they went as far as to attempt to arrest one of our men, in this act; went on and passed several hot springs, and camped on a cold one. came 20 miles

Tuesday 10th

Started at six, during the day quitted the valley of the great salt lake but were still in the midst of many settlements. came 16 miles

Salt Lake City (1851)
[*Library of Congress/James Ackerman*]

Wednesday 11th

travelled near the borders of the lake again in the midst of farms etc [*near Ogden, Utah*]. Came 15 miles

Thursday 12th

Started at nine, camped at 1, bought some good watermelons & laid by the balance of the day, Elsworth bought 15 bushels of potatoes at 1 dollar per bushel, all other vegetables in the same ratio

Friday 13th

Started at six, at noon forded Weber river, there were several houses here, and the river was studded with willows, in the afternoon had a very heavy rain. came 14 miles

Saturday 14th

started at ten, the cause of this late starting was that we lost some of our cattle among the willows. they were at last found. camped and made 15 miles

Sunday 15th

Started at six, weather very pleasant, camped on box elder creek [*near Brigham, Utah*], here we found many berries of different varieties. grass rather scarce

Monday 16th

went on two miles and camped the balance of the day, killed a beef which we divided, grass abundant. came 2 miles

Tuesday 17th

Started at six, very hot day, nooned at bear river [*near Corinne, Utah*], road good, camped at old spring, grass scarce. came 17 miles,

Wednesday 18th

Started at six, camped at the salt cold sulphur and warm springs. this is pretty much of a curiosity, weather cool & pleasant, came & made 13½ miles. had to go 15 miles for fresh water

Thursday the 19th

Started at six. Struck Deep Creek during the day. Camped at 5 oclock. The Weathers has been remarkably pleasant to day. Saw some Antelopes but we could not get a shot at them, these animals are very shy. Came 20 miles today.

Friday the 20th

Started at six, some of the loose cattle were missing but Elsworth said that there was no water for 20 miles ahead, we could not wait and leaving 3 men to hunt them up we Started. Weather rather hot, saw more antelope today. Shot him in the Leg but he escaped. Came this day 20 miles Without Water.

P. S. The men returned with the Stray Cattle during the night.

Saturday 21st

Started at 7 oclock. Camped at 5 oclock. Weather disagreeable & Windy, nothing of Interest occurred today Except breaking a yoke. Came 15 miles

Sunday 22nd

We laid by all day to rest our Cattle. Killed an antelope which was divided among us. Came 0 miles

Monday 23^{d}

Laid by all morning. 11 men left the train today "disgusted" with our slow progress to pack on their backs. They took 5 horses with them to be used for packing. They walking meanwhile. It was a novel sight to see them depart from camp. Started at 11 oclock. Camped on Story Creek. The road has been rather rough. Came 13 miles

OLD MODES OF LOCOMOTION.—THE PACK-HORSE TRAIN.

[*©iStock.com/duncan1890*]

Tuesday 24th [*Dominique's 11th birthday*]

Started at six. Struck the Goose Creek and Camped on it at 4 oclock, to morrow we will have to cross the Goose Creek mountains, "breakers-ahoy" [*danger ahead*]

Wednesday 25th

Started at six, had a very mountainous road over the "Goose Creek Mountains." Camped at 4 oclock. Weather delightful. Made 14 miles

Thursday 26th & friday 27th

Started at 7 oclock, road level, camped a few hours at a small spring where grass was very scarce. we hitched on the cattle and it being moonlight we travelled on in search of water and grass. I and many others went on ahead, we passed many trains and many cattle, we saw ^{some} by the side of the road fatigued broken down and starving, we that were on horseback reached the water full 2 hours before the train. we lit a large fire with sagebrush to warm ourselves the weather being rather chilly. here there was no grass, the train came on but the cattle had nothing to eat, two had been left behind, it was midnight, laid by till five oclock, I slept not a wink. the cattle were flying in all directions in search of something to appease their hunger, we at last succeeded in huddling them together and at five oclock again passed on, the cattle could hardly be made to go, they were dreadfully cut and whipped by the merciless drivers. and no one rode within the wagons. all that had not horses were forced to walk, we camped at noon where there was no water and not much grass. here we left the cattle roam far from camp with guards. Elsworth said there was no water for 8 miles ahead. some who had horses went back to the last camp a distance of 5 miles and watered their horses. but this was too much for the cattle, we dug a well and got a little dirty water for 125 head of cattle. it would not do. came including 1 day, 1 night until 12, and then started at 5 till 12. 34 miles

Saturday August 28th

Started at 5, had not proceeded more than 1 mile when we found innumerable small springs of clear & cold water. this proved that Elsworth was unacquainted with the road. here we unhitched the cattle, our horses drank about 4 buckets of water each & might have drank much more had we not restrained them. the cattle dirtied all the springs in their hurry to drink, some also got stuck in the mud, after they had enough we again hitched on and went on a few miles near some more fine springs and camped, where grass was in abundance. came 6 miles

Sunday August 29th

Started at 7, camped at one, where grass was again in plenty as well as water and camped at 1 oclock, laid by the balance of the day.

Monday August 30th

started at six, entered thousand springs valley at 11 oclock [*northwest corner of Utah*], we saw springs of all varieties cold, sulphur, alkali, poison, and some so hot that a person could not put his hand in the water two minutes without being scalded. some washed their clothes in the springs, grass around was abundant. passed a large mormon train returning to Salt lake, camped at a large spring clear as crystal and as cold as ice, it is about forty feet in circumference but we could find no bottom. came 18 miles

Tuesday August 31st

Started at six, road very rough, passed a creek whose waters were the color of limy water. the water was not wholesome to drink. we soon expected to reach Humboldt or Mary's river [*a tributary of the Humboldt River*], camped at five near a spring. came 16 miles

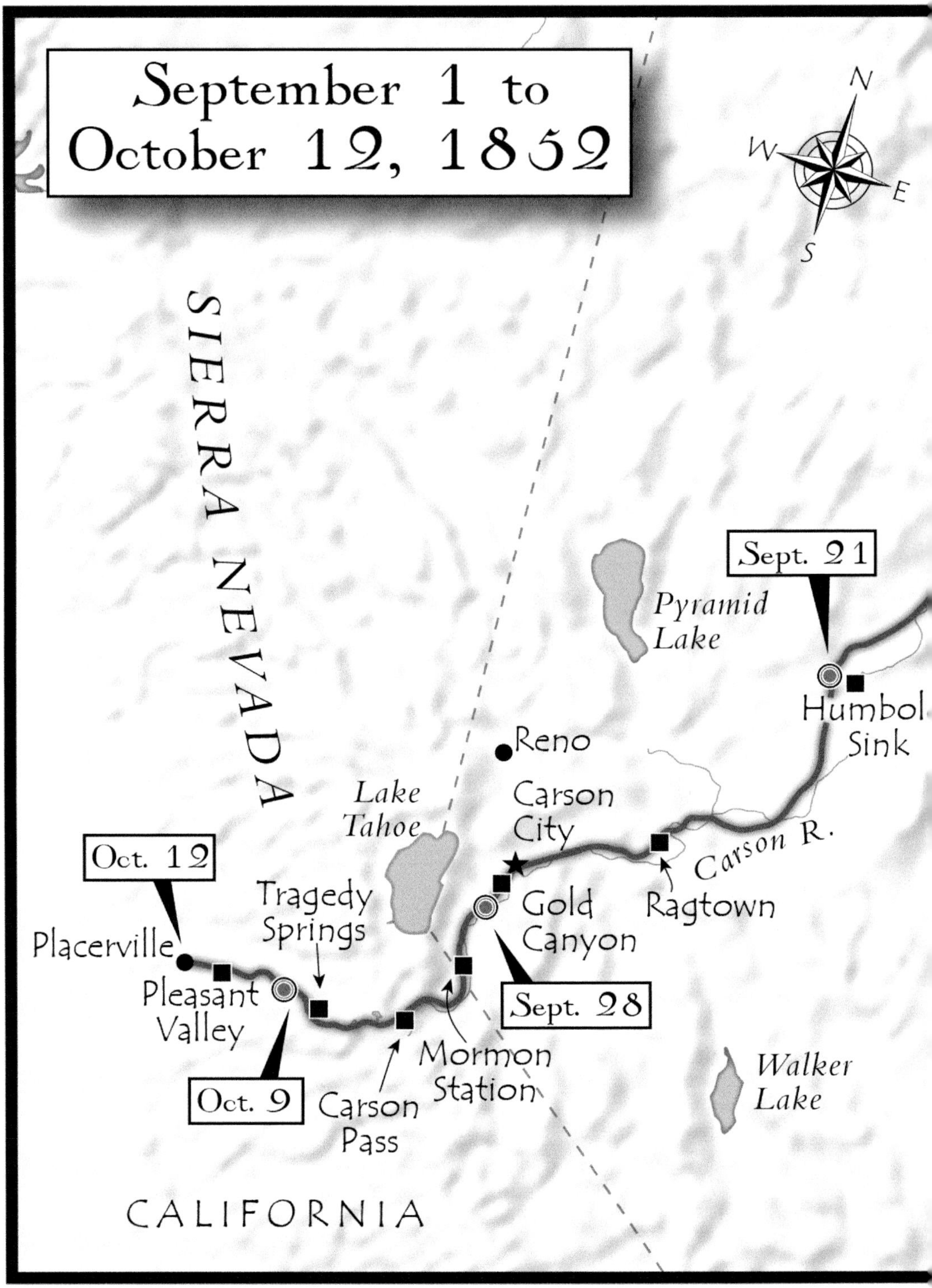
September 1 to October 12, 1852
N
W
E
S
SIERRA NEVADA
Pyramid Lake
Sept. 21
Humbol
Sink
Reno
Lake Tahoe
Carson City
Carson R.
Ragtown
Gold Canyon
Oct. 12
Placerville
Tragedy Springs
Pleasant Valley
Sept. 28
Mormon Station
Walker Lake
Oct. 9
Carson Pass
CALIFORNIA

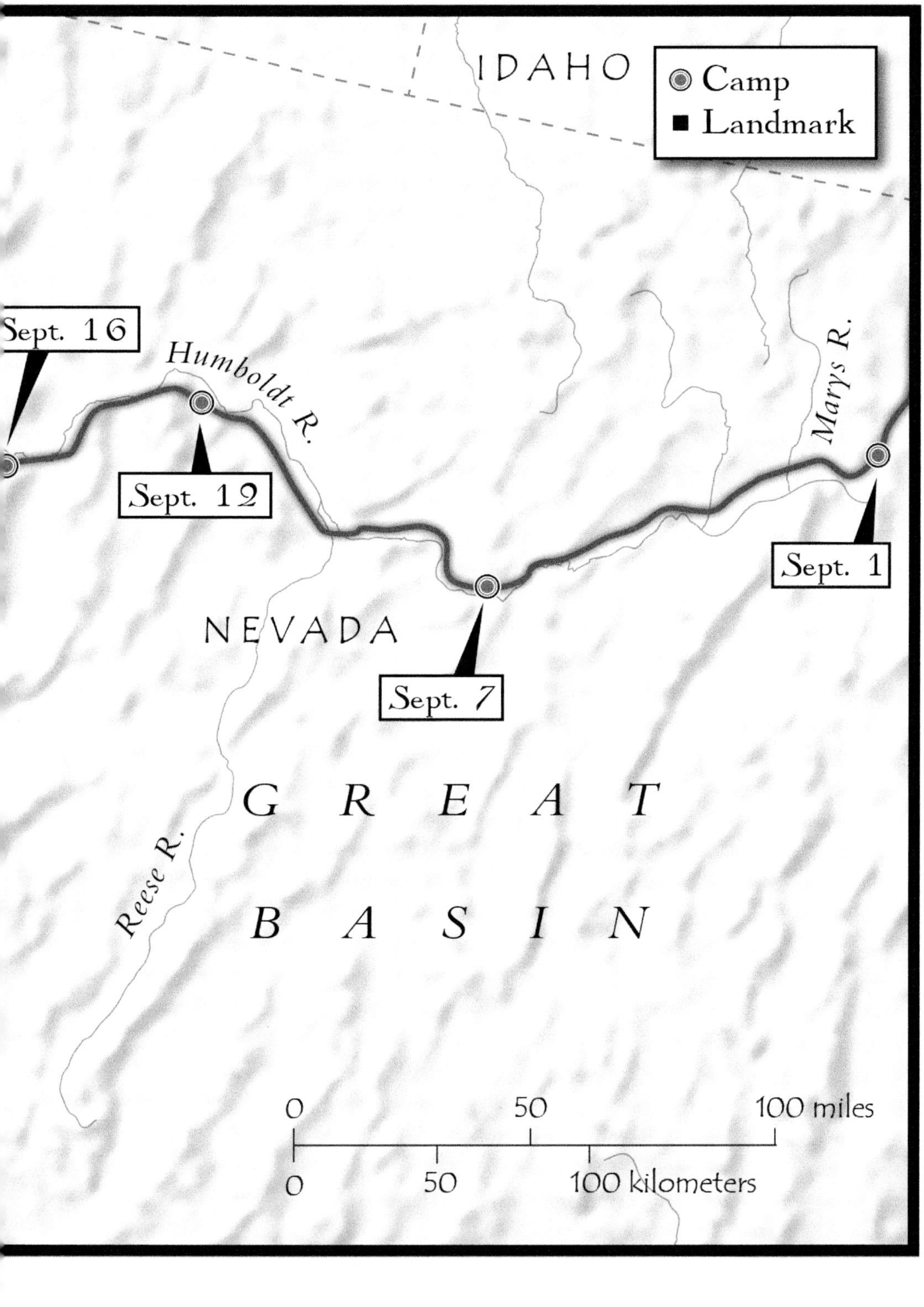

[Marin History Museum/Mary Rostad]

Wednesday September 1st 1852

started at 7. at noon reached the Humboldt river [*they had now entered Nevada*], the water was scanty in the river at this point, it was studded with willows. many say that the waters of this river is bad and poisonous but we believe they are in error, it tasted as well as any water we ever drank, in the distance we saw the Humboldt river mountains, weather very pleasant, struck our tents and eat our meals for the first time on the Humboldt river. came twenty miles.

Early American Pioneers Arriving in Nebraska, 1856

[*©iStock.com/bauhaus1000*]

Thursday September 2nd

Started at 6. forded Humboldt river, father killed about 8 ducks and captured a young eagle, grass abundant, this is seldom, but this year the river had risen in spring & overflowed the banks which caused the fine grass our cattle enjoyed to grow in abundance. came 16 miles.

Friday September 3rd

Started at six. still followed the Humboldt which we are destined to pursue several hundred miles. heard rumors that indians had robbed trains on ahead of us. we now resolved to place plenty of guards around the camp at night to watch the cattle. the river was so thickly bordered by willows that it could not have surprised us much at seeing indians among them. camped at 6. came 16 miles

Humboldt River Valley (1859)
[*Library of Congress/Daniel A. Jenks*]

Saturday September 4th

this morning the cattle were scattered in all directions through the willows and it was 10 oclock before they were all found. we then travelled on and camped at six the camping ground being nearly always alike, killed some more ducks. came 16 miles

Sunday September 5th

started at 8. In the forenoon met many returning californians mostly packers, they gave us a california newspaper. and gave us some news of California, they thought we could not go over the mountains the "Sierra Nevada's", this season and believed we would be forced to spend the winter in Carson's Valley. camped by the side of a trading post where several of the cattle were exchanged for fresh ones. came 19 miles

Monday September 6th

Started at 8. Camped at one, killed a beef which was divided among the train, the manner in which the good & bad pieces were disposed of to the different wagons was as follows. one man shut his eyes and turn his back, while another sings out "for who is this?" and the other calls back the number he pleases. came 14 miles

Daily Alta California.

VOL. III. SAN FRANCISCO, FRIDAY MORNING, JUNE 18, 1852. NO. 169.

Express Lines. | Steamers Advertised. | Vessels Advertised. | For Sale—To Let. | Watches and Jewelry. | Business Directory.

Daily Alta Newspaper June 18, 1852
[*California Digital Newspaper Collection, Center for Bibliographic Studies and Research, University of California, Riverside, http://cdnc.ucr.edu*]

Tuesday September 7th

laid by all morning until 1 P.M when we travelled on without any thing of occurrence, we camped at a bend in the form of a horseshoe [*East of Carlin, Nevada*]. one of our horses got loose, we had much trouble to retake him, we left an ox behind who would not travel. came 11 miles

Wednesday Sept 8th

Started at six, weather pleasant & warm. killed many ducks this day, passed two trains one of six and the other of eight wagons, camped at five. came 20 miles

Thursday September 9th

Started at six, camped at 4, made 14 miles, in our camp we found a human scull. Wether that of an indian or white man none of us knew as we were ignorant of Phaesiology [*physiology*].

Friday September 10th

Started at six, weather hot and road very dusty, travelled slowly, a large train passed us the Tenessee train, camped at five. came 16 miles

Saturday September 11th

Started at six, found this morning that two horses were gone, they were no doubt stolen by the Diggers or Apaches,[22] one train that we met stated they had had five stolen the night before. Elsworth was unconsolable, he left Collins behind to search after the horses. Collins was a good fellow and on many occasions saved Elsworth's cattle from peril. he was an irishman by birth—and had entered the train & engaged himself as driver of loose cattle, he was expert in this line, a thing which all drivers of cattle ought to be, camped at 4 oclock. made 17 miles

Sunday September 12th

Started at six, camped at six, nothing particular worthy of occurrence occurred this day. came 14 miles

Monday September 13th

started at 8, left the Humboldt to the left and ascended a high sand ridge, and travelled in the sand to make a cutoff, again camped on the Humboldt [*near Golconda, Nevada*]. came 16 miles

Early American Pioneer Western Wagon Train, 1868

[*©iStock.com/bauhaus1000*]

Tuesday September 14th

laid by all day, killed an ox, we made a net and commenced to drag the river for fish. we did not catch many, I and some others took a swim in the river. we had much fun to day, several of the men resolved on the morrow to go to California afoot.

Wednesday September 15th

Thirty men left us today a foot for California. they bore about forty five pounds each on their backs. they started at six oclock, & we at 9 oclock, camped at six. came fifteen miles [*near Winnemucca, Nevada*]

Thursday Sept 16th

started at six, halted at ten & commenced to cut grass for the cattle. there being no grass between this point & the sink of the Humboldt river, by the aid of schythes [*scythes*], we cut some dry grass & stowed it in and behind the wagons.

The way we had now to pursue was along the sandy bluffs of the Humboldt to the sink, we resolved to travel on the south side, camped where the grass was very scanty. came 17 miles [*near Imlay, Nevada*].

Cutting Grass with a Scythe
[*Winslow Homer, Metropolitan Museum of Art, Bequest of Miss Adelaide Milton de Groot (1876–1967), 1967*]

Friday September 17th

Started at seven, went over a high sand ridge and camped adjoining a trading post where we had some more cattle exchanged, here we had a little grass but not enough for the cattle, we had recourse to the grass we had cut. came 15 miles.

Saturday Sept 18th

road again very sandy & dusty, started early during the afternoon, I & Elsworth went on ahead to find a camping ground, we were quite lucky, the train was some five miles behind. As I have said before there was wide sandy bluffs on both sides of the river, between these bluffs far below the river flowed in large bends, with considerable difficulty Elsworth descended below and in about ¾ of an hour he returned, told me he had found good grass and water below, and sent me back towards the train yet about three miles back to give the train notice to come this way & we camped on the high bluff overlooking the river, while we drove the cattle & horses below where they regaled themselves well. came 14 Miles [*near Lovelock, Nevada*].

Sunday Sept 19th

Started at six, at two we arrived at the "Meadows," where there was abundance of grass, there being large prairies rolling with grass. here we camped, could only get water but from wells dug in the vicinity. there were about five hundred wagons around us, recruiting their cattle to cross the desert, and were cutting enormous masses of grass for the cattle on the desert, came 8 miles, weather fine & hot. Collins the driver returned this day, he had the 2 horses which we had supposed to be stolen by the indians. he found them in a train.

"Crossing the Prairie"

[*Overland in 1846: Diaries and Letters of the California-Oregon Trail, Dale Morgan, University of Nebraska Press, 1993*]

Monday September 20th

Still continued to lay by. cut much grass which was to be used for the cattle on the desert, we also filled all our cans & Barrels with water. the dessert we had to traverse was fifty miles long without grass & water and the last twelve miles of the road was sand, there were many snakes around, but none I think that were poisonous, we killed many.

Tuesday September 21st

left 7 wagons behind, Elsworth sold them to a trader, as also some cattle, therefore we had only 6 wagons left, an easier number to travel with. two more men started a foot to day. Elsworth gave them $10 each, we started at seven, at two oclock reached the sink of the Humboldt river, the sink was a large lake whose waters were alkali & poisonous, we went on a little further and camped on the edge of the dessert. there was a little grass here. there was also a trading post ~~here~~, we resolved to travel on the Carson route.[23]

Wednsday Sept 22nd 1852

&

Thursday 23rd

started at 7, in a half an hour we were on the dessert road very even and hard, stopped at noon about an hour, gave our cattle a little grass, and then again went on, saw many animals dead by the side of the road, and some on the point of dying, again halted at four oclock. P.M. at our stopping place we saw many broken vehicles, again we fed our cattle and travelled on by moonlight, the cattle were commencing to be exhausted. we stopped again at midnight one hour & the night was very chilly. I was on horseback enveloped in a blanket, here we gave the cattle all the grass we had, as well as water we being then twelve miles from Carson's river [*see End Notes for Carson's biography*][24] but we had the worst road to travel, the balance being deep sand, as I have before stated-again started at 1 a.m & with the loss of two cattle we reached carson's river at eight P.M. when yet within ¼ of a mile of the river the cattle were full of vigor & life & were sometimes trotting. there is no doubt but that they scented the water, we camped at ragtown [*now a ghost town on U.S. route 50*]. the town combined contained 4 trading posts, they sold provisions at an enormous high price, Carson river is about as fine a stream as we ever crossed, the water cold as ice and as clear as crystal. we drove the cattle about two miles on the right hand side of the dessert, here there was plenty bunch grass. came 50 miles

Friday September 24th

Started at 1 P.M travelled along the banks of the Carson river, passed the United States station at 4, we inquired for provisions. but they had none. We now lived on crackers & beans. Gen. Raines of the U. S. station paid us a visit. Camped at six. Made 12 miles

Saturday September 25th

Started early & passed a large pike county train, camped at three, slaughtered a fine beef that Elsworth bought at a trading post. drove the cattle across the river where there was good grass. made a large fire in the night, weather pleasant. Came 19 miles

Sunday September 26th

Started at six, roads very mountainous and sandy, passed by some tall mountains, we took a cutoff, camped again on Carson river. Came twenty miles

Monday September 27th

Started early and came over a twelve mile dessert road, very sandy & dusty, camped on the carson [*near Dayton, Nevada*]. Came eighteen miles

Tuesday September 28th

Stated at eight, passed Gold Canõn at two P.M. This is a small settlement & Gold Canõn derives its name from the fact that there are gold mines in the vicinity [*on the border of Sierra and Nevada counties*].[25] Camped & made 16 miles

Wednesday September 29th

Started at 7, soon reached the Eagle Ranch where we camped. weather during the day foggy; & disagreeable, we were now in carson's Valley [*Carson City, Nevada*] & at the base of the Sierra Nevada mountains, there was plenty of grass & wood, many wagons were camped here. Came 10 miles

Thursday September 30th

Started at 6, at three P.M. reached the mormon station [*established by the Mormons to aid emigrants*] & camped, we saw a considerable number of houses erected in the vicinity of the station, they had not and sold no flour at the station, we bought some Beef, Pork, Tea, & sugar, & Beans. came this day 15 miles, the weather this day was very fine & cool, the Sierra Nevada is covered with snow

Friday October 1st 1852

Laid by all day to recruit the cattle for to cross the mountains. Also cut grass

Saturday October 2nd

Started at eight, a twelve commenced to have a very rocky road, camped at 4, the snow falling heavily meanwhile. Came 11 miles [*near Fredericksburg, California*]

Sunday October 3rd

Still snowing, started at 9, had to travel a road that if not seen cannot be described over rocks three feet high, one wagon had to be taken about a hundred feet & then stop to bring on the other and so on, at every moment the wagons were expected to upset & go to pieces, we were now in the Canñon [*Carson River Canyon, near Alpine Village, California*], it stopped snowing at 2 oclock, road continued to get worse. stopped for the night under tall fir trees, came during the whole day 4 miles

CROSSING THE SIERRAS.

[©iStock.com/duncan1890]

Recreation of Mormon Station in 1958
[*National Park Service*]

Monday October 4th

started early, passed red lake & commenced to ascend the little summit. It was very steep & encumbered with immense rocks, we had to take up wagon, by wagon, we hitched 10 yoke of cattle on each wagon, never had we been in worse passages, we at last reached the little summit & rested there about two hours when we again pushed on. a large flock of sheep passed us, went on and camped on the borders of a large lake. I know not it's name [*Caples Lake in Alpine Valley, California*], we sent the cattle about two miles from camp where there was good grass. Came 18 miles

Tuesday October 5th 1852

Still laid by, killed some very fine ducks on the lake, there was a trading post near our camp inhabited by Canadians.

Wednesday October 6th

started at 7, we were now at the base of the big summit, it took us 4 hours to ascend, it was higher but not so steep as the little summit, snow here was a foot deep, we found a negro man frozen to death by the cold and snow, he had belonged as we heard to Pepbles train. camped on the banks of a small creek where there was but little grass. Came 14 miles

Early American Pioneer Covered Wagon with Oxen, 1868

[*©iStock.com/bauhaus1000*]

Thursday October 7th

Started at eight, met a trader of whom we bought 100 pounds of flour & 75 pounds of Pork, camped at 4, drove the cattle in a rich valley below where there was grass in abundance as well as water there being a fine lake [*Silver Lake*], came fourteen miles, road was roses to what we saw a few days before although bad now

Friday October 8th

started at 12 Oclock & arrived at the tragedy springs where we camped,[26] we drove the cattle about two miles below where there was good grass, it was on the same lake they had been the night previous, came 7 miles, road always bad

Saturday October 9th

Started at nine. Mrs. Boyle a lady of wagon No 1 being insulted by Elsworth, threw a fire brand [*a stick of burning wood*] at him. he tamely submitted to this, camped at [Leu] spring, grass scarce, made 14 miles, killed two deers

Sunday October 10th

Arrived at the intersection of the Volcano road [*a road to Volcano, California—either Pioneer-Volcano Road or Pine Grove–Volcano Road*], we followed the placerville train, passed a house & camped at 3 oclock P.M, made 12 miles, fed our cattle with barley

Feeding the Teams on the Placerville Route (1866)
[*Library of Congress/Lawrence & Houseworth*]

Monday October 11th

arrived at Pleasant valley at twelve oclock, from here we quitted the train for ever and taking a spring wagon we went on towards placerville, slept for the night at Weaverville

Tuesday October 12th

arrived at Placer ville, here I worked about three weeks at mining, my partner was Collins, we got along very well with each other. It was with much sorrow I parted from him on leaving Placerville for San Francisco about the 1st of November 1852.

John M. Verdenal
Dominique Verdenal

Placerville, California (1849) [*University of California, Berkeley Library*]

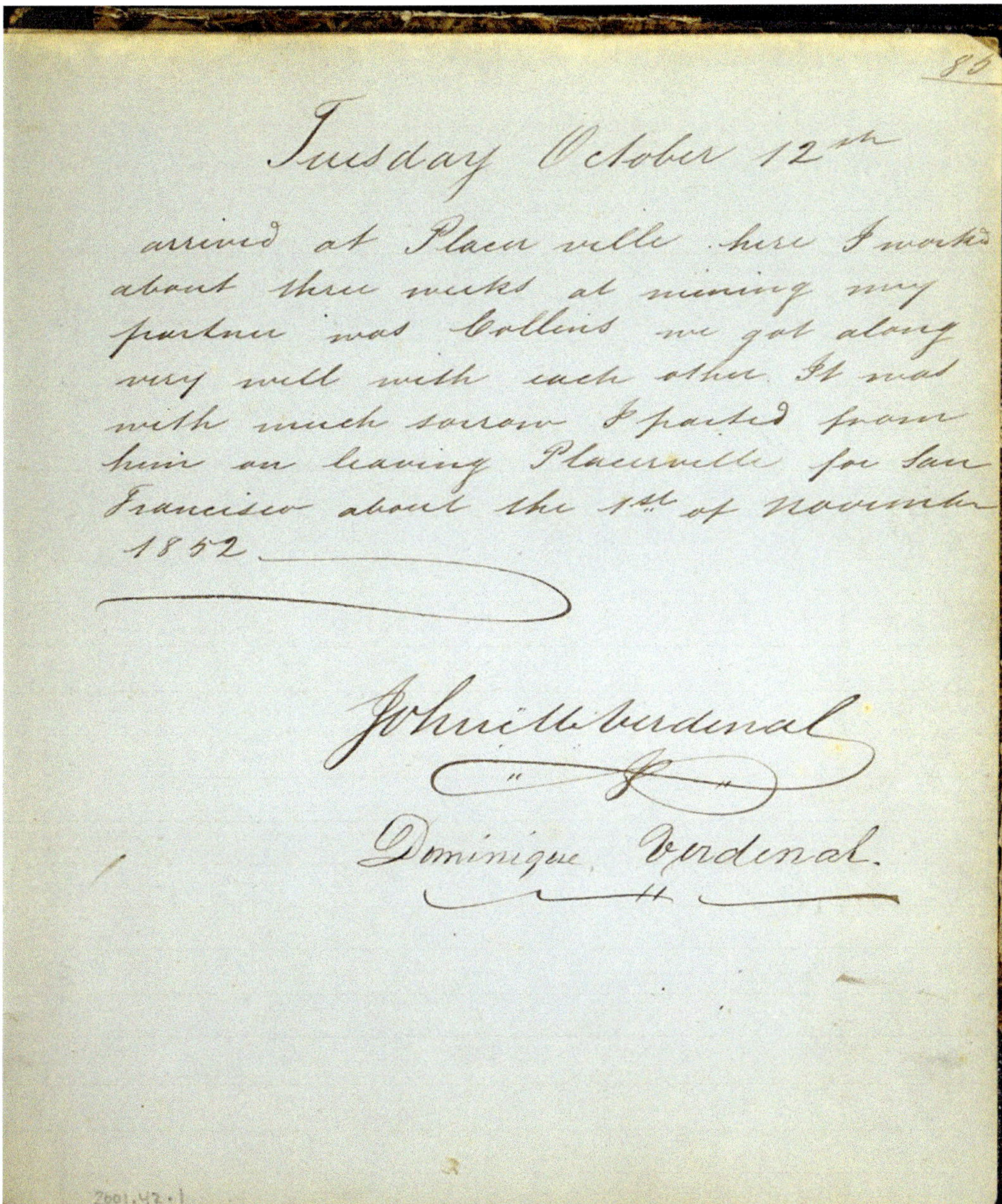
85

Tuesday October 12th

arrived at Placerville here I worked about three weeks at mining my partner was Collins we got along very well with each other It was with much sorrow I parted from him on leaving Placerville for San Francisco about the 1st of November 1852

John M. Verdenal

Dominique Verdenal.

2001.42.1

[*Marin History Museum*]

THE VERDENAL FAMILY BIOGRAPHIES

This chapter presents biographies of the brothers and their parents. Additional information about other descendants can be found at www.MarinHistory.org.

JEAN BAPTISTE VERDENAL
(~1808– March 22, 1871)
FRANCOISE (REISET) VERDENAL
(1820–February 25, 1862)

Jean Baptiste Verdenal
[*The private collection of Frederick and Elizabeth Walker*]

Françoise (Reiset) Verdenal
[*The private collection of Frederick and Elizabeth Walker*]

Jean Baptiste Verdenal's birth year is uncertain, probably between 1803 and 1808. He was born in France, as were his parents and grandparents who reportedly came from Bremenil, Meurthe-et-Moselle, Lorraine, France. Approximately ten miles northwest of Bremenil lies the village of Verdenal. Unfortunately, the connection between the family name and the nearby village has been lost to history.

Sometime before 1839, Jean Baptiste arrived in New York City. On January 26, 1839, he married nineteen-year-old Françoise Reiset, also from France. Their marriage certificate reflects their Americanized names: John and Frances. There is no record of whether they knew each other in the old country. In December of that same year, Frances gave birth to their first son, John Martin, in or near Utica, New York. Their second son, Dominique François, joined the family in 1841. Two years later, John Baptiste was granted naturalized United States citizenship, confirming he had lived in the United States for a minimum of five years and New York state for at least one year.

John Baptiste's occupation, as listed in the 1850 St. Louis, Missouri Census, was "coffee house." Given the family's mixed neighborhood of merchants (i.e. furniture dealers and a liquor purveyor) as well as laborers (i.e. carpenter, painter, and bricklayer), he might have owned, or simply worked at, a local coffee house.

Without his sons' journal, we would not have known that John Baptiste and family traveled from St. Louis, Missouri, to Placerville, California, in 1852. Eight years later, the 1860 San Francisco Census recorded him as aged fifty-four, living with his wife, two sons, and three other adults from Sonora, Mexico, and France. The census is silent on whether the additional adults were boarders, servants, or relatives.

While attending university in St. Louis, John Martin sent his mother an affectionate and newsy letter—in French. Possibly Frances never learned to read English or the family spoke French at home.

John Baptiste appeared in an 1861 San Francisco city directory working at a bakery. A year passed and Frances died in late January at age forty-two while her sons attended Harvard University. She was buried at Lone Mountain Cemetery in San Francisco. In the early 1900s, San Francisco closed most of the cemeteries within the city limits, citing sanitation and hygiene risks. Mrs. Frances Verdenal was reinterred at Cyprus Lawn Memorial Park, ten miles to the south.

1870 found John Baptiste living with his youngest son, Dominique, and his wife, Susan. His oldest son, John, was also in residence. Surprising for a man over sixty years old, he described his occupation as stone cutter. John Baptiste Verdenal died in his late sixties, on March 22, 1871, at 1234 Dupont Street in San Francisco. After crossing an ocean by ship and a continent by prairie schooner, he lived to see his college-educated sons living and working side-by-side with lawyers, bankers, and capitalists.

JOHN MARTIN VERDENAL, SR.
(December 24, 1839–December 11, 1914)

John Martin Verdenal was born on Christmas Eve, 1839, in Utica, New York. John's parents, John Baptiste and Frances (Reiset) Verdenal, had emigrated to New York from France in the early 1800s. Twenty months later, the birth of John's brother, Dominique François, completed the family.

For reasons unknown, the Verdenals moved from New York to St. Louis, Missouri, where the boys attended school. In April 1852, when John was twelve, they departed St. Louis on the El Dorado wagon train headed for Placerville, California. During the six-month journey, John and Dominique made notes of each day's events.

After John tried his hand at gold mining in Placerville with little reported success, the Verdenal family settled in San Francisco. The brothers attended St. Ignatius Academy, founded in San Francisco in 1855. When John turned eighteen, he returned to St. Louis to study at

John Martin Verdenal Sr. and Jane (Lawler) Verdenal
[*Marin History Museum*]

St. Louis University. In a September 1858 letter to his mother (in French), John reported he was "twice as strong" as when he left California. He boasted of studying mineralogy, architecture, Latin, and Greek, up to six hours a day. Given his class on the planets, he made special note of a comet that appeared among the stars every evening that fall (the Donati comet, the first comet photographed). John was eager for news from home and complained that his younger brother had visited France without him. "Dominique wins and I lose."

Donati's Comet
[*William Turner, Yale Center for British Art, Paul Mellon Collection, B1975.4.1767*]

Dominique joined John at St. Louis University during John's sophomore year. Both brothers graduated in 1861 with degrees in philosophy, after which they attended Harvard University in Cambridge, Massachusetts. While the Civil War raged to the south and classmates left to join the fight, John and Dominique remained at their studies, graduating with law degrees in 1862.

The next year, the California Supreme Court, recognizing John's license to practice law in Massachusetts, admitted him to the bar in California. Early San Francisco newspaper advertisements promoted John's offices at 636 Clay Street, later at 405 Kearny Street in the heart of downtown San Francisco, and finally, as the twentieth century began, at 314 Montgomery Street. As advertised in local newspapers, including the Italian language publication, *Italia*, John's services were extensive: "divorces, probating, bankruptcy, collections, suits, title perfected, documents drawn, mortgages, property bought, money loaned and insurance offered at 30c on $100."

The same year he began to practice law and fifteen years after gold was discovered at Sutter's Mill, John started speculating in mining companies. Over time, he bought shares in the Marble Valley Gold and Silver Mine, the Brennus Gold and Silver Mining Company, the Redan Silver Mining Company, and the Chieftain Gold Mining Company. Not all of John's mining ventures glittered with precious metal. In 1868, he and his associates sued The Tuolumne Mountain Gold and Silver Mining Company for the rich sum of $1,484 in damages and $10 in costs ($31,000 and $210 in 2019). Eventually, in 1886, John's interest in mining led him and colleagues to launch a new magazine: *Miners' Advocate.*

John's business investments were not limited to mining. In 1870, the City of San Francisco granted him and a handful of allies the rights "to lay down and maintain a street railway along and upon various streets." San Francisco smartly required the new railway barons to first "plank, pave or macadamize" the roads on which they planned to lay their rails, giving the growing city not only tax revenue but surfaced streets and public transportation too.

As an engaged and respected member of the business community, John's most frequently reported civic duties included planning festivities. He, along with others, pledged to support a traveling opera singer whose earnings were taken to pay her theatre's debts. Back when the Fourth of July was celebrated with near religious fervor, he regularly participated in organizing committees. Alongside Charles de Young, Editor-in-Chief of the *San Francisco Chronicle,* John coordinated the city's salute to the placement of the Golden Spike, signaling the completion of the Transcontinental Railroad.

John regularly spoke at the Knights of Pythias and political party events, including a Thirteenth Senatorial District dinner where the speeches were described as mercifully "brief and covered fully the main questions of the campaign" including the "Chinese problem" and the "water question." Where John stood on the issues of the day is unknown. John was also recognized as a Commander in the local American Legion. In short, there does not seem to be a community organization in which John *was not* active, often at a senior level. It is worth noting he participated in the Knights of Pythias's fraternal and benevolent functions for two decades, longer than any of his other commitments.

John's engagement in Republican politics began strong and deep. A founding member of the Young Men's Republican Club, he was several times a delegate for the Party convention, was nominated in the state primary and served as a marshal in Grant's Invincibles—a Republican Marching Club. His name regularly appeared in the newspaper alongside fellow lawyers supporting various candidates for judgeship. In June 1871, John's election ticket included "a colored citizen"—a bold and progressive move. Predictably for the times, John's ticket lost. John came into his own the following year when he was elected Township Justice by the San Francisco Board of Supervisors, as well as Justice of the Peace.

Political life was not all elections, dinners and marching. On April 19, 1871, William Higgins, a rival contender in the primary, attacked John in the Mint Saloon on Commercial Street in San Francisco. Struck in the face, John bled freely. Higgins and another man then drew pistols and threatened to shoot him. John escaped into the street and Higgins was arrested.

John married Jane Lawler in 1875. They had three children: Cora Francoise (1878), Grace Mayfield (1879), and John Martin Jr., or Jack (1884).

In 1877, John came in second for City and County Attorney after W. C. Burnett, a frequent co-counsel. The result could have been awkward except for the fact that John knew he had lost before he had begun. The *San Francisco Chronicle* newspaper noted how, at a campaign event, the eventual winner (W. C. Burnett) was modest and quiet. "He knew that J. M. Verdenal took the nomination without any expectation of being elected..." Talk about taking one for the party.

Although a Republican stalwart for a decade, John changed parties in 1881 to become a Vice-President of the local Democratic Party. Perhaps he grew tired of losing elections, or bar fights had lost their charm, or possibly his ideology had evolved. Nevertheless, it did not take long for John to stand for election as a Democratic candidate for the Board of Education. There is no record of John winning that election either.

Of French ancestry, John surely did not have the luck of the Irish. On St. Patrick's Day, 1883, while crossing Market Street from the Palace Hotel, he was trampled by two runaway horses and a milk wagon. He was thrown "fifteen feet, turning a summersault in his flight and striking with a thud on the pavement." Seriously injured and unconscious, John was taken to his home at 608 Guerrero Street in today's Mission District. After three days and against his doctor's expectations, he awoke and eventually recovered.

The Palace Hotel *c.* 1887
[C.P. Heninger]

John moved his family across the Golden Gate to San Rafael in Marin County in 1905. In April 1906, an earthquake shook the region, nearly burning San Francisco back to sand and swamp. That same year, three years after Dominique's namesake son died, John's twenty-one-year-old son, Jack, had been sent to Tucson under doctor's orders for his respiratory problems. Caught in a rainstorm, he took a chill and died within hours.

Although he never practiced law again, John became a fixture in Marin County political circles. He served as an election officer, Deputy District Attorney, and as Real Estate Commissioner, appointed by his daughter Grace's husband, Thomas Patrick Boyd.

On Friday, December 11, 1914, John Martin Verdenal Sr. died at the age of seventy-five, surrounded by his family. His passing was unexpected as John had complained of stomach troubles for only a few days. His obituaries described him as a prominent attorney, a fine scholar, well-read, and very refined. The *Marin Journal*, given to sentimental language, proclaimed, "John M. Verdenal, one of California's pioneer jurists, was called last Friday to appear before the Omnipotent Judge, whose jurisdiction is the infinite." Funeral services were held at his home at 6th and C Streets. He was laid to rest next to his son at Mount Tamalpais Cemetery in San Rafael, California.

John Martin Verdenal Sr. (1839–1914) m. Jane E. Lawler (1856–1941)

<table>
<tr><th>Children</th><th>Grandchildren</th><th>Great-Grandchildren</th></tr>
<tr><td>Cora Francoise Verdenal
(1876–1919)</td><td>Never married</td><td></td></tr>
<tr><td rowspan="8">Grace Mayfield Verdenal
(1879–1960)
m.
Thomas Patrick Boyd Sr.
(1872–1933)</td><td>Grace Elizabeth "Betty" Boyd
(1903–1995)
m.
James Owen Orr
(1901–1967)</td><td></td></tr>
<tr><td rowspan="2">Frances Verdenal Boyd
(1905–1995)
m.
John Daniel McDonald Jr.
(1904–1985)</td><td>Mary Margaret "Dolly" McDonald
(1930–2013)</td></tr>
<tr><td>John Daniel McDonald III
(1937–2005)</td></tr>
<tr><td rowspan="3">Ruth Isabel Boyd
(1908–1993)
m.
Frank Preston Nibley Sr.
(1907–1995)</td><td>Frank Preston Nibley Jr.
(1934–2014)</td></tr>
<tr><td>Thomas Boyd Nibley
(1936–?)</td></tr>
<tr><td>Nancy Ann Nibley
(1939–2013)</td></tr>
<tr><td>Thomas Patrick Boyd Jr.
(1914–1985)</td><td></td></tr>
<tr><td>John Martin "Jack" Verdenal Jr.
(1884–1906)</td><td>Never married</td><td></td></tr>
</table>

DOMINIQUE FRANÇOIS VERDENAL SR.
(August 24, 1841–February 6, 1916)

Dominique François Verdenal was born in Utica, New York, to John Baptiste and Françoise (Reiset) Verdenal, French immigrants. Dominique's middle name, the male version of his mother's birth name, Françoise, continued the family tradition of naming children after their parents, often using their mother's maiden name. His brother, John, was a twenty-month-old toddler when Dominique arrived.

Sometime before 1850, the family moved to St. Louis, Missouri, where the brothers attended school. In 1852, ten-year-old Dominique and twelve-year-old John traveled with their parents in a prairie schooner from St. Louis, Missouri, to Placerville, California.

From that youthful start as an author, writing became a defining characteristic of Dominique's future. In California in 1856, he published *The Pacific Youth*, the "first amateur journal that appeared on the (west) coast." Editor D. F. Verdenal was fifteen years old.

At preparatory school in San Francisco and again at university in St. Louis, the brothers remained classmates. Dominique chronicled his experiences in a new diary from 1858 to 1861, beginning with his twenty-four-day sailing journey from San Francisco to New York City, with an overland train trek across Panama.

The sights of New York delighted Dominique. Manhattan was a "splendid city in the way of the number of fine buildings, numerous public squares, parks ... the bay is spacious ... steeples upon steeples arise towering to the murky skies—mingled with the lesser temples of religion and art." He praised the city's grand mansions, sleek sailing ships, fine restaurants, and world-class theatre. "The stage of America has produced some of the greatest actors of modern times. Need we cite ... Booth, Huen—and many others whose names are legion." One wonders which of the theatrical Booth family Dominique considered a great actor—Edwin, Junius or Lincoln's future assassin, John Wilkes.

Dominique arrived in St. Louis in November 1858. His university reading list was prodigious: arithmetic, algebra, grammar, Greek, various histories, and geography. School was not all lectures and learning. One morning he woke to snow, "the first real snow I've seen for seven years ... the ground seems invested with a mantle of innocence—so pure in its whiteness." With apparent glee, he recorded, "snowballing is the order of the day."

On occasion, his diary mentions John, such as the three times they were chastised for talking in study hall and the time they received money from home to fund their vacations and wardrobes.

Contemporary photographs show Dominique bearded and dressed in a dark suit and ribbon tie. After graduating in 1861 from the University of St. Louis with degrees in philosophy, the brothers visited Washington, D.C. At the Capitol, according to Dominique, "we saw nearly everything of consequence." They attended debates and met Senators and Congressmen. They toured Mount Vernon, the Patent Office and were "disappointed at the

Smithsonian Institute." Having seen all there was to see, they traveled north to graduate school at Harvard University in Cambridge, Massachusetts. They graduated with law degrees in 1862. Upon their return to San Francisco, they practiced law and became active in the political and business events of their time. Occasionally, the brothers acted as co-counsel in estate cases and in support of a lady's breach of promise suit.

Dominique Françoise Verdenal
[*Kimberley Henson*]

Where John's interests focused on politics and clients, Dominique became active in the mining community, serving as secretary to an expanding number of mining companies from his offices at 327 Pine Street in downtown San Francisco. Some say he tried wildcat mining himself; one observer commented Dominique was as facile with a spade as a pen. Others described him as an eloquent speaker, noting he was "frequently interrupted by vociferous applause." In August 1868, he spoke in support of Ulysses S. Grant for president. The event advertisement ends with a commitment certain to please San Francisco's women, "Front seats will be reserved for Ladies. By order of the Committee."

Dominique married Susan Shannon Edelen in 1869; they were both twenty-seven years old. Attending a political ball in Sacramento later that year, Susan was described as "pretty as a picture in a silver-spangled tarlatan of spotless white looped with white roses ... she was much admired." Their three children continued the use of parent's names as middle names: Charlotte Francis "Lottie" (1870), Blanche Edelen (1876), and Dominique François, Jr. "Frank" (1877).

Susan Shannon Edelen
[*Kimberley Henson*]

Dominique's youthful wavy hair was tamed as he aged. The full beard of his early years became a Van Dyke moustache and goatee, accompanied by wire-rimmed pince-nez glasses balanced on his nose. In Dominique's letters to the editor, he protested being misquoted, once declaring the *San Francisco Examiner* newspaper libelous in its reporting. He appeared before San Francisco's Board of Supervisors offering to "plank the sidewalk on Buchanan Street, between Washington and Jackson" streets, an oddly altruistic offer since he had no obvious connection to the property. Another appearance was to protest the regrading of Sutter Street between Gough and Octavia. In the late 1870s and early 1880s, Dominique lived near the corner of Sutter and Octavia.

In 1872, the *Stockton Daily Independent* described Dominique as the "Sacramento correspondent of the *San Francisco Chronicle*," the first mention of what would become a decades-long writing career. As most authors know, writing does not always pay the bills. That same year, with a family to support, Dominique added "Stock Broker" to his collection of occupations including lawyer, author, land speculator, and mining company secretary. Around that time, Dominique and two colleagues published the *Stock Exchange*, "the only genuine stock journal" in San Francisco whose "articles are ably written and, at the same time, spicy and readable." Continuing his journalistic efforts, Dominique became the first editor of the *San Francisco Chronicle* newspaper, launched in 1869 by Charles De Young and his brother Harry.

Dominique Françoise Verdenal
[*Kimberley Henson*]

In 1880, Dominique and family moved to West 45th Street in New York City, to establish a newspaper similar to the *Stock Exchange* he had published in San Francisco. That same year, the United States Census listed thirty-nine-year-old Dominique as a resident of New York City with an occupation of Secretary of Mines.

Later that decade, newspapers referred to Dominique as "the New York correspondent of the *Chronicle*" and "the New York mining correspondent of the *S. F. Chronicle*"—a logical assignment given his long history as a mining secretary. Many of Dominique's Sunday columns, under the sobriquet "Verdenal's Chat," focused on the social lives of prominent Californians in New York City. In what must have been a gold mine of future articles, Dominique established a Pacific Coast Visitors' Exchange at 45 Broadway, allowing visitors to "acquire information regarding the metropolis and transact business generally." In 1900, after two decades as a *Chronicle* columnist, Dominique's byline also appeared in the *Examiner* newspaper over the boastful claim, "Special by leased wire, the longest in the world"—a brag in desperate need of an exclamation point.

In 1889, Dominique financed a play written by an unknown playwright, although he would allow "it is the work of one of (San Francisco's) well-known society women." Given Susan's later published novels and plays, we might guess she wrote the play her husband funded. Dominique's secrecy might have been a ploy to protect his wife if her play flopped. If Susan was the author, the experience must have encouraged her. Her stage comedy, *The Laughing Girl*, was presented in San Francisco in 1893. Her romantic novel, *Ladies First*, "full of the flavor of the old mining and stock gambling days of California" was published in 1896.

Susan regularly traveled by train from New York to visit her daughter Charlotte, then Mrs. William Forsyth, at their vineyards in Fresno, California. An 1891 newspaper, on the other hand, noted Dominique as absent from the West Coast for twelve years. It was not until 1896, sixteen years after he had moved to New York, that newspapers recorded his return to San Francisco.

NEW BUSH-ST. THEATER.

M. B. LEAVITT.............Lessee and Proprietor.

A DECIDED SUCCESS!

MISS CLARA LIPMAN, LOUIS MANN

AND COMPANY

In MRS. D. F. VERDENAL'S Three-act Comedy,

THE

LAUGHING GIRL

MATINEES THURSDAY AND SATURDAY.

[*San Francisco Call, November 27, 1893*]

In New York, Dominique and family lived in the Dakota apartments on the corner of 72nd Street and Central Park West. Since construction on the sold-out Dakota was completed in 1884, only two years before the family's residence is first noted, the Verdenal family may have been original tenants of the now historic apartment building. While Dominique did not travel to California, he returned to Washington, D.C., in 1893 to attend Grover Cleveland's inauguration as twenty-second President of the United States.

On May 4, 1903, Dominique and Susan's son Frank died in the unfortunately named town of Comfort, Texas. Neither the cause of his death nor his reason for being in the state were reported. Twenty-five years old at the time of his death, Frank's wife and infant daughter survived him. Three years later, brother John also lost his namesake and only son. Once again, the brothers shared a life experience, this one surely crushing.

In 1914, the same year John died, Dominique retired from writing. He and Susan departed New York to split their days between their two Fresno-based daughters, Charlotte and Blanche, spending the summer months in cooler San Francisco. The California pioneer, influential in the creation of the San Francisco newspaper profession, died at age seventy-four on February 8, 1916, at Charlotte's home. Susan outlived her husband by fifteen years.

The Dakota Apartments *c.* 1890
[*Library of Congress/Courtesy of Museum of the City of New York*]

Dominique Françoise Verdenal
[*Kimberley Henson*]

<table>
<tr><td>Dominique François Verdena
(1841–1916) l</td><td>m.</td><td>Susan "Susie" Shannon Edelen
(1842–1931)</td></tr>
<tr><th>Children</th><th>Grandchildren</th><th>Great-Grandchildren</th></tr>
<tr><td rowspan="3">Charlotte Francis "Lottie" Verdenal
(1870–1957)
m.
William Forsyth
(1850–1910)
m.
Dan Brown Jr.
(?-?)</td><td>Donald William Forsyth
(1892–1951)
m.
Mary Louisa Wynn
(1892–1973)</td><td></td></tr>
<tr><td>Dorothy Verdenal Forsyth
(1894–1933)
m.
Arthur Silcock Lindley
(1893–1954)</td><td>Dorothy Forsyth Lindley
(1933–2006)</td></tr>
<tr><td>Richard Lanham Forsyth
(1900–1982)
m.
Jane Warner
(1908–1991)</td><td></td></tr>
<tr><td>Blanche Edelen Verdenal
(1876–1935)
m.
Lee Lincoln Gray
(1870–1924)
divorced
~1915</td><td>Austin D. Gray
(1898–1925)</td><td></td></tr>
<tr><td rowspan="2">Dominique Francois "Frank D." Verdenal
(1878–1903)
m.
Alice Haddon Owston
(1882–1971)</td><td rowspan="2">Francis Owston Verdenal
(1903–1989)
m.
Phillip Osborne Hoag
(1899–1953)</td><td>Verdenal H. Hoag
(1924–2017)</td></tr>
<tr><td>Susan Hoag
(1927–1963)</td></tr>
</table>

Endnotes

1 El Dorado: the "gilded one" also a city or country reported to hold fabulous riches. The family's destination of Placerville, California is the county seat of El Dorado County.

2 The boys often wrote "ss" as "fs," also known as a "long s." As reported in the *Oxford Companion to the Book* (2010), the long s had fallen out of favor in quality London printing after 1800 but continued in handwriting into the second half of the nineteenth century.

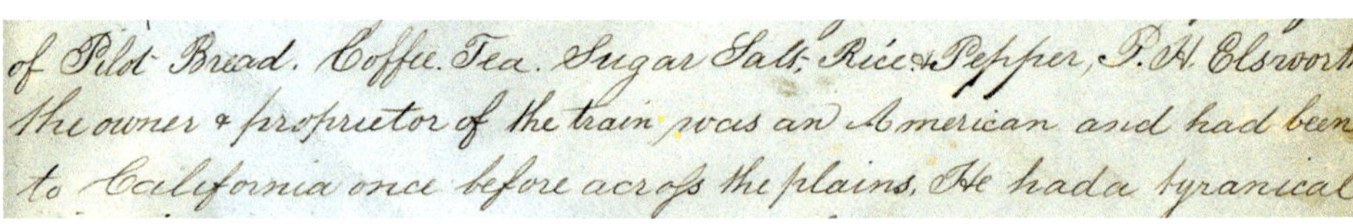
of Pilot Bread, Coffee. Tea. Sugar Salt, Rice & Pepper, P. H. Elsworth
the owner & proprietor of the train was an American and had been
to California once before acrofs the plains, He had a tyranical

Long S in "acrofs"
[*Marin History Museum*]

3 N.B.: Observe carefully or take special notice (used in written text to draw attention to what follows). Also written as *nota bene*—Latin for "note well."

4 Recruit: to strengthen or reinforce, from the French "recruiter" (17c.)

5 The main Oregon Trail crossed the Kansas River at Topeka, so the El Dorado wagon train must have turned south at Big Springs onto the Union Ferry Branch to cross farther west.

6 The Jesuits founded St. Mary's Mission in 1847 to "civilize" the Pottawattamie Indians driven from the Great Lakes area. In 1855, the town of St. Mary's developed around the old mission.

7 The Big Blue River is the largest tributary of the Kansas River, joining it just east of Manhattan, Kansas. The crossing is known as Independence Crossing.

8 That the wagon train followed the Blue River is confusing. The Oregon Trail ran northwest from Independence Crossing, while the Blue River runs northeast to Marysville. About a day's journey beyond the crossing, the trail encounters the Little Blue River. Perhaps John thought the Little Blue River was the Blue River.

9 In 1848, the United States Army established Fort Kearny in honor of General Stephen Watts Kearny (1794–1848).

10 Later travelers continued for sixty miles up the south bank of the South Platte and crossed farther upstream at the Lower California Crossing. The El Dorado train apparently crossed just upstream of the confluence, in the current city of North Platte.

11 Court House Rock is located six miles south of the current Bridgeport, Nebraska. In 1841, a traveler wrote, it "commands a view of the country for forty miles around and meets the eye of the traveler for several successive days, in journeying up the Platte."

12 Chimney Rock National Historic Site is located four miles south of current Bayard, Nebraska. After examining over 300 pioneer journals, historian Merrill Mattes determined that Chimney Rock was the most-mentioned landmark.

13 Probably the trading post run by mountain man Major Andrew S. Dripps or possibly one nearby run by the French fur trader Joseph E. Robidoux.

14 A ferry was built in 1850 to prevent the loss of life of emigrants trying to cross the Laramie River. In 1852, the ferry was replaced by a crude bridge. Emigrants frequently complained about the high tolls.

15 Holmes D. Van Schaick, an eyewitness from another train, described the hanging as occuring at LaBonte Creek.

16 Lafayette Tate (~1833–June 15, 1852). Nineteen-year-old Lafayette Tate might have been another nameless California settler had he found a different way to defend his brother.

Lafayette's brother brawled with the cattle overseer of the Brown wagon train in June 1852, according to David J. Langum's article, "Pioneer Justice on the Overland Trails" for the *Western Historical Quarterly* 5 (1974). Lafayette ran to his brother's rescue, stabbing the overseer in the back. Lafayette then "turned him over and caught hold of his hair and cut his throat and deliberately wiped the blood from his knife on the grass" (Diary of Caroline Richardson, June 15, 1852).

The armed brothers fled but a hurriedly assembled posse tracked the fugitives down. Upon their return, prairie justice was enacted. A judge, jury, witnesses, and counsels were sworn in. The jury speedily declared Lafayette guilty. The spectators, more mob than audience, hanged him within thirty minutes.

Roughly three weeks later, the Verdenal brothers passed Lafayette's intentionally shallow burial site. "... we noticed his grave from which one of his bones protruded forth and his hair was strewed around the grave. It was a shocking sight."

17 Independence Rock State Historic Site, fifty miles southwest of Casper, Wyoming, is as tall as a five-story building and covers twenty-seven acres. Heavily inscribed with pioneer names, the rock has been called "the great register of the desert." It got its name because emigrants figured they needed to be at least to this point by Independence Day if they were to get over the mountains before winter. The El Dorado train was twelve days behind this schedule.

18 Devil's Gate is a gorge on the Sweetwater River in Wyoming, five miles southwest of Independence Rock. The actual route of travel did not pass through the narrow cleft.

19 On July 24th, they were at "Parting of the Ways," fifteen miles northeast of Farson, Wyoming. The main trail to Oregon went to the right. The left fork went to Salt Lake City and California. Most travelers to California and Utah turned onto the Sublette Cutoff, established by Caleb Greenwood in 1844, avoiding the Little Colorado Desert.

20 Jim Bridger.

James Felix Bridger was born March 17, 1804, in Richmond ,Virginia, the second son of James Bridger and Chloe Tyler Bridger. When Jim was eight, the family headed west, settling in Six-Mile Prairie, just across the Mississippi from St. Louis. The boys never attended school. Bridger remained illiterate all his life.

James Felix Bridger
[Gates Frontiers Fund Wyoming Collection within the Carol M. Highsmith Archive, Library of Congress, Prints and Photographs Division]

When he was thirteen, his mother Chloe died, followed by his father and brother William. He was bound as a blacksmith's apprentice. At eighteen years old, he joined a beaver-trapping expedition to the upper reaches of the Missouri. After five months of labor, they reached the Yellowstone River and built Fort Henry. Bridger joined a group of trappers led by Jedediah Smith to try to find a way over the Rockies. On Bridger's twentieth birthday, they were the first white men to discover South Pass in Wyoming. This pass would become the route of the California and Oregon Trails. The next year, traveling alone, he discovered the Great Salt Lake. He was probably the second white man to see Yellowstone. He trapped beaver and wandered the mountains for fifteen years. He married a Flathead Indian woman named Cora. They had a daughter, Mary Ann, in 1836 and a son, Felix Francis, in 1841.

By 1843, the beaver trade had collapsed and the great migration of settlers to the west had begun. Bridger built a trading post and blacksmith shop on the Green River to serve the wagon trains. The post became known as Fort Bridger. In 1845, they had another daughter, Mary Josephine; Cora died later that year. In 1847, the Mormon Pioneer Party stopped at Fort Bridger. Bridger suggested Brigham Young investigate some fertile land east of the Great Salt Lake.

The next year Bridger led a Shoshone war party against the Utes and returned with a Ute bride. In 1849, with the Gold Rush flooding the trail, his second wife died delivering a fourth child, Virginia. Later that year, he married Little Fawn, daughter of the chief of the Shoshones. They had a son, John, in 1850, and a daughter, Elizabeth, in 1852. That year the Mormons attacked and burned Fort Bridger. Bridger and his family barely escaped to Westport, Missouri, where they bought a house. In 1858, the army hired Bridger as a scout in the war between Utah and the United States. By the time he returned to his home, Little Fawn had died after giving birth to another son, Bill.

Bridger worked as an army scout through another ten years of bitter Indian fighting. He retired in 1868 when his eyesight started to fail—by 1875 he was blind. He died on July 7, 1881.

21 At Fort Bridger they left the Oregon Trail and took the Hastings Cutoff toward Salt Lake City. The cutoff was promoted by Lansford Warren Hastings (1819–1870) in his 1845 guidebook, though he apparently never attempted it himself. The Donner party followed his advice and found the road so difficult they were late crossing the Sierra, resulting in their disaster. In later years, the cutoff was improved and became a popular route.

22 "Diggers." A derogatory term for several desert Indian tribes who dug roots for food. In this case, these were probably Paiutes. The Apaches did not live in Nevada.

23 The California Trail divided at the Carson Sink. The Truckee Trail (roughly today's Interstate 80) ascended the Truckee River to Wadsworth, Nevada. The Carson Trail (roughly today's U.S. 95) ascended the Carson River to Ragtown, Nevada.

24 Kit Carson.

Christopher Houston Carson was born December 24, 1809, in Madison County, Kentucky. His father, Lindsay Carson, had fought in the Revolutionary War, the War of 1812, and the Indian Wars. Lindsay and his second wife, Rebecca Robinson, along with their fifteen children, were attending a Christmas Eve dinner party at a neighbor's home when Rebecca went into labor. The baby was so small he was given the nickname Kit that night.

When Kit was one year old, the family moved to Boone's Lick, Missouri, where they lived on land belonging to the sons of Daniel Boone. When he was eight, his father was killed by a falling tree. Four years later, his mother remarried.

Kit did not get along with his stepfather and moved to Franklin, Missouri, where he apprenticed to a saddler. The work did not suit him. When he was eighteen years old, he signed on as livestock handler with a caravan on its way to Santa Fe, then in Spanish territory. Kit liked the area and settled in Taos. He learned the skills of a trapper and woodsman and acquired Spanish and several Indian languages. With mountain men Jim Bridger and Bill Williams, he went on several hunting and trapping expeditions throughout the west, reaching as far as Los Angeles and Sacramento.

Christopher "Kit" Carson (1860-1875)
[*Brady-Handy photograph collection, Library of Congress, Prints and Photographs Division*]

For ten years, Carson trapped in the Rocky Mountains, often hunting down and killing Indians. In later years, as he learned more about Indian language and culture, he became more sympathetic and urged the government to give them reservations of their own. In 1836, he married an Arapahoe woman named Singing Grass. After she died in the birth of their second daughter, Carson married a Cheyenne woman, Making-Out-Road. After she divorced him, he married a fourteen-year-old Mexican girl, Josefa Jaramillo, in 1843. Together they had eight children.

In 1842, Carson met John Fremont, a United States Army officer on an expedition to explore and map the west. Fremont hired Carson as a scout and guide. Over the next two years, they mapped the Oregon Trail to the Pacific Coast. In 1845–1846, Fremont and Carson were mapping in Northern California when the Bear Flag Revolt broke out. Fremont assumed charge of the revolt. He and Carson captured San Rafael and San Francisco and claimed the territory from Mexico for the United States.

In 1848, Carson carried word of the gold strike to Washington, D.C. Carson's adventures and Indian fighting made him a national hero and the subject of numerous books and "dime novels." He continued his scouting work and killing Indians until the Civil War when he joined the Union Army and was made a colonel. He led the First New Mexico Volunteer Infantry against the Confederates at the Battle of Valverde in 1862.

Carson later fought the Apaches and the Navajos and was responsible for massacres of entire villages. He died at Fort Lyon, Colorado, on May 23, 1868, aged fifty-eight.

25 Gold mining began in Gold Canyon in the early 1850s at the German Bar, Independent, and Gold Cañon mines.

26 The Carson Trail was established in 1848 by members of the Mormon Battalion returning to Salt Lake City from the war in California. Three of their scouts were murdered at this spring on June 27, 1848.